T0347405

Access Services:
The Convergence of Reference and Technical Services

Forthcoming topics in *The Reference Librarian* series:

• Access to Western European Libraries and Literature: In the Spirit of 1992, Number 35

Published:

Reference Services in the 1980s, Numbers 1/2
Reference Services Administration and Management, Number 3
Ethics and Reference Services, Number 4
Video to Online: Reference Services and the New Technology, Numbers 5/6
Reference Services for Children and Young Adults, Numbers 7/8
Reference Services and Technical Services: Interactions in Library Practice, Number 9
Library Instruction and Reference Services, Number 10
Evaluation of Reference Services, Number 11
Conflicts in Reference Services, Number 12
Reference Services in Archives, Number 13
Personnel Issues in Reference Services, Number 14
The Publishing and Review of Reference Sources, Number 15
Reference Services Today: From Interview to Burnout, Number 16
International Aspects of Reference and Information Services, Number 17
Current Trends in Information: Research and Theory, Number 18
Finance, Budget, and Management for Reference Services, Number 19
Reference Services and Public Policy, Number 20
Information and Referral in Reference Services, Number 21
Information Brokers and Reference Services, Number 22
Expert Systems in Reference Services, Number 23
Integrating Library Use Skills into the General Education Curriculum, Number 24
Rothstein on Reference . . . with some help from friends, Numbers 25/26
Serials and Reference Services, Numbers 27/28
Weeding and Maintenance of Reference Collections, Number 29
Continuing Education of Reference Librarians, Number 30
The Reference Library User: Problems and Solutions, Number 31
Government Documents and Reference Services, Number 32
Opportunities for Reference Services: The Bright Side of Reference Services in the 1990's, Number 33
Access Services: The Convergence of Reference and Technical Services, Number 34

Access Services:
The Convergence
of Reference
and Technical Services

Edited by
Gillian M. McCombs

The Haworth Press, Inc.
New York • London

Access Services: The Convergence of Reference and Technical Services has also been published as *The Reference Librarian*, Number 34, 1991.

The Haworth Press, Inc., 10 Alice Street, Binghamton, NY 13904-1580

Library of Congress Cataloging-in-Publication Data

Access services: the convergence of reference and technical services / Gillian M. McCombs, editor.

    p. cm.

Includes bibliographical references.

ISBN 1-56024-170-5 (acid free paper)

1. Reference services (Libraries)—Automation. 2. Library science—Technological innovations. 3. Processing (Libraries)— Automation. 4. Information technology. 5. Libraries and readers. 6. Reader guidance. I. McCombs, Gillian M.

Z711.A167 1991

025.5'24—dc20

91-35637

CIP

Access Services:
The Convergence of Reference
and Technical Services

CONTENTS

III. THE NEW ACCESS SERVICES

SPECIAL REPORT

ABOUT THE EDITOR

Gillian M. McCombs, BA, ALA, is Assistant Director for Technical Services and Systems at the University of Albany, State University of New York. She was educated in England and received her library degree from Leeds Polytechnic. Ms. McCombs has written numerous articles on the public/technical services interaction as well as library leadership, popular culture and the role of practising librarians in library education. She is currently a member of the LAMA Publications Committee, the ALA Committee on Accreditation Site Visitor Pool and a Past-President of the Eastern New York Chapter of ACRL.

Introduction:
The Reference/Technical Services Interaction, Revisited

One of the most identifiable trends in the information field today is the changing emphasis from collections to access, from document description to document delivery. The focus is moving from bibliographic access to information access, providing information itself rather than information on information. This trend necessitates a change in service orientation and attitude which is redefining the traditional roles of reference and technical services.

The Fall/Winter 1983 volume of *The Reference Librarian* addressed the relationship between these two functional areas, put them into a historical context, and made some suggestions for future directions. It is now time to see how accurate those predictions were, whether or not there is still a "problem,"[1] as Gordon Stevenson called it, and to see if there has been any progress made toward what the majority of us have to agree is our communal goal — the provision of access to the world of information, whatever our patron frame of reference.

The automation of library processes has moved very definitely from the 'backroom' of technical services to the 'front desk' of reference services. Online catalogs are the norm rather than the exception. Migrations to second and third generation systems are almost as common as first time installations. The prediction made almost twenty years ago at the 1973 ALA preconference "Library Automation: The State of the Art II," and cited in the earlier-mentioned issue of *The Reference Librarian*, that "The fast-response, computerized union catalogs and their ancillary network apparatus, will do more to change our goals and attitudes, believe it or not, about *library service* than it has or will change our cataloging pro-

1

cedures"[2] is now a fact. User expectations have increased dramatically. Reference librarians are performing a very different kind of service than they were 20 years ago. However, in spite of AACR2, catalogers are still cataloging very much the same way they were when OCLC came into being, only now transposing the contents of a 3" × 5" card onto an 8" × 11" screen. Bibliographic description performed inhouse still focuses on the contents of a library's local holdings, which may today only represent a small portion of the information to which the library is providing access, underscoring the emphasis on collections rather than access.

This volume of *The Reference Librarian* will take a look at what this trend means — for librarians, for services and for patrons. Articles range from topics such as cross-training experiments, revised organizational structures, the new role of the bibliographic utilities, library school education for the redefined professional, changing philosophy in the profession, radical suggestions for change in cataloging codes and the implications of these changes in the broader context of total information access and national information policy.

Whatever other conclusions may be drawn from this volume, it seems clear Gordon Stevenson's fear, in 1983, that "widespread and radical change seems rather unlikely in the near future,"[3] may well be proved happily wrong. Many of the scenarios predicted in 1983 are now taking place in our libraries. The 1990s will truly test our fortitude, creativity and ability to harness change for the successful completion of our mission. To that end it is imperative that public and technical services redefine both their own roles and their relationship in order to provide the services needed by patrons through the year 2000.

Gillian M. McCombs

REFERENCES

1. Stevenson, Gordon. "The Nature of the Problem, If It Is a Problem." *The Reference Librarian*, No.9, Fall/Winter 1983, pp.3-7.
2. Martin, Susan K. and Brett Butler. *Library Automation: The State of the Art II*. Papers presented at the Preconference Institute held at Las Vegas, Nevada, June 22-23, 1973. Chicago, American Library Association, 1975. 191p.
3. Stevenson, Gordon. Op. Cit.

I. PUBLIC SERVICES PERSPECTIVE

Dual Function Librarianship: What Makes It Work?

Amy L. Paster

SUMMARY. With the growth of automation and decline of catalogers, dual function librarianship is becoming a more attractive option for medium to large sized libraries. Background information and advantages and disadvantages are discussed for two variations of dual function librarianship: the divisional plan and decentralized cataloging. The University of Nebraska successfully used the divisional plan for twenty years without the aid of automation. For the past six years the Pennsylvania State University Libraries have utilized decentralized catalogers largely due to the support of the administration and the automation of technical services.

Automation and integrated online computer systems are today the two most frequently cited reasons behind the combining of public and technical services in libraries. Economic factors and a shrinking pool of catalogers are two other driving forces behind this trend: "In recent years it has become almost impossible to recruit and employ full-time catalogers under any circumstances."[1] "Libraries are increasingly facing unprecedented difficulties in recruiting and

Amy L. Paster is Life Sciences Reference Librarian/Cataloger, Pattee Library, Penn State University, University Park, PA.

retaining professional catalogers.''[2] These two quotes were written almost thirty years apart from each other; some things never change. The first quote is by Frank Lundy from the University of Nebraska, which solved its cataloging dilemma by initiating a plan called the divisional concept. The second quote is by James Neal, formerly of Pennsylvania State University. Penn State solved its problem by the partial decentralizing of the cataloging department.

CONCEPTS

The divisional concept in librarianship bases organization and service on subject rather than on function. Frank Lundy developed and evolved the subject divisional plan from what was originally a building concept at Nebraska to a philosophy of library service based on improving the student's ease of access to library materials and services.[3] One outgrowth of this concept was the dual-function or dual-assignment librarian.

Decentralized cataloging is similar to the divisional plan in that it is a division based on subject rather than on function. The driving force behind the change at Penn State was automation. No longer was it necessary to have all the catalogers, tools, and support staff in one centralized location. Original cataloging could be performed at the public service units. A second factor crucial to Penn State's success with decentralized cataloging is continued administrative support for non-traditional organization.

UNIVERSITY OF NEBRASKA

In the 1950s, libraries were becoming intensively interested in organizing general library services by subject matter. This interest grew because of changes in educational philosophy — recognition of the value of wider and more intensive reading and the decline of the "single text" course. At this time most libraries operated under the closed stack principle. With the growing student population this became impossible to maintain and open shelving became the norm:

Barriers between books and students were removed by placing the books on open shelves in large enough quantity to reflect the entire undergraduate curriculum, including books of general interest as well. And the word "books" was reinterpreted to include all forms of print immediately pertinent to the program, that is, books, periodicals, pamphlets, reference sets, and so on. These were brought together not by format and process, but by content and idea. Large workable collections were brought together by subject matter to serve groups of related departments of instruction — hence the phrase divisional plan.[4]

With this plan in place, the next step was staffing. It was desirable to hire public service librarians with subject expertise in the specific areas outlined by the plan. It was also important to have librarians with subject expertise in the technical service units to solve difficult problems in the cataloging and classification of the material. Duplication of effort and staff could not be afforded, i.e., hiring one science specialist for public service and another one for technical services.

Divisional Plan

In 1951 the University of Nebraska initiated a system of dual-assignment librarianship. Staff in these positions were recruited on the basis of subject matter knowledge as well as librarianship. Responsibilities included reference work with students and faculty, selection of materials, and full cataloging and classification of new materials appropriate to the division involved. By 1954 the Catalog Department was staffed with three full-time catalogers and eight half-time junior catalogers. The full-time catalogers handled administrative duties, original cataloging, and the training and revision of the junior catalogers. The junior cataloging staff was comprised of people from each subject division: two from the humanities, two from the social sciences and two from science and technology, plus one each from the libraries of the Colleges of Agriculture and Law. Each junior cataloger spent half the work week cataloging.[5]

The divisional library plan was used through the 1940s and 1950s (Figure 1).[6] By the early 1960s some aspects of the plan were in trouble. Student enrollment grew from 8,700 to 20,000 in the space

FIGURE 1

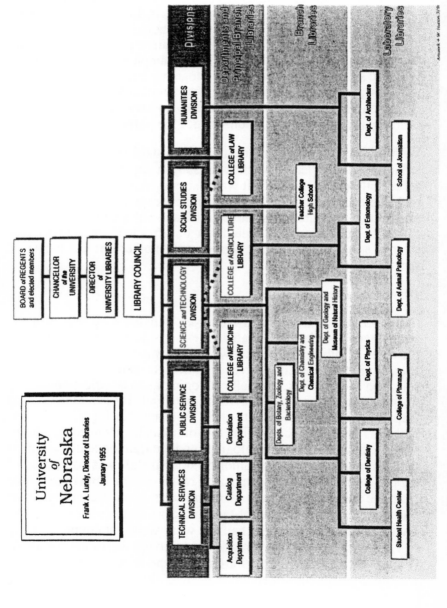

of one decade. The teaching faculty also expanded in order to keep pace with climbing enrollment. The amount of material to be processed greatly increased with the information explosion, which in turn led to a severe space problem for both collections and patrons. Library staffing did not grow sufficiently to keep up with those changes, and in the mid-1960s hours and services had to be cut back. The subject reading rooms that had been established earlier in the plan had to be abandoned in order to concentrate more hours of service at still fewer public service areas. Later on, book collections were combined to form a College Library Collection with the traditional reference and periodicals rooms.

By the beginning of the 1970s the physical aspects of the divisional plan were gone.[7] The University of Nebraska Library is currently organized along the traditional public services-technical services division and no longer employs dual function librarians.

It is probable that more than one factor contributed to the demise of the dual function position at Nebraska. Unlike many academic libraries in the sixties and seventies, Nebraska did not enjoy expanding university support.[8] This critical factor, together with the increase in the materials processing load, the increase in student and faculty demand for services, and the primitive state of library automation, put untenable pressures on the original cataloging staff. Responding to these pressures, the library administration abandoned the Dewey classification system in favor of cataloging from Library of Congress copy and eliminated the dual function librarian position. Administrative support had been effectively withdrawn from the divisional library concept.

THE PENNSYLVANIA STATE UNIVERSITY

The Penn State University library began as a library for the Farmer's High School in 1857. There were sixty-nine students enrolled and one hundred and ninety volumes in the library that first year. Since then the library has grown to over three million volumes, and the school to 70,000 students.

The first professionally trained librarian was not hired until 1924. Minimal requirements for librarians were established in 1935; these included graduation from an accredited college and at least one year's additional training in library science. The first steps toward automation were initiated by Ralph W. McComb in the 1950s.[9]

The Penn State University Libraries are currently comprised of a central collection (Pattee) and six subject libraries: Earth and Mineral Sciences, Mathematics, Engineering, Physical Sciences, Life Sciences, and Arts. There are also libraries at each of the twenty campuses throughout the Commonwealth. Collections include over three million volumes, as well as extensive holdings of maps, microforms, rare books, special collections, and documents. Serving approximately 70,000 students at all locations, with 35,000 enrolled at University Park, (home of the Pattee Library) the Libraries have developed an integrated, automated system called LIAS (Library Information Access System). This system controls interactive functions such as record creation/maintenance and inventory control, which includes circulation, personal reserve and intra-campus lending.

The Libraries at University Park are organized along the traditional public services-technical services model. Staffing of the technical services unit under manual technology (card catalogs) was hierarchical, largely due to its size and rapid growth, and also highly centralized. Because of the steady growth of shared cataloging in the 1970s, there was a shift in focus from the professional librarian to the large clerical and paraprofessional staff, who performed the bulk of the department's work.

Automation

Penn State made an early commitment to automation. System specification documents were being written in 1975 with the actual implementation being done in a number of stages. In 1981 the input system was expanded to support current online cataloging and database maintenance, and it was at this time that the card catalog was closed. This new development had a tremendous impact on the technical services division. To capitalize on the similarities between functions, the existing processing staffs for copy cataloging, acquisitions searching, and retrospective conversion were combined. During this same period the professional staff were spending up to sixty percent of their time working on documentation and training for the new system.

By the end of the transition period, the availability of shared cataloging had increased to the point that original catalogers had lost touch with a significant portion of the work flow through the department. The professional staff felt they had lost their role as bibliographic experts and policy makers. There was also a problem with the clerical staff: though productive, they found the work to be regimented and fragmented. While it can be said that automation was partially to blame for these problems, without it the dual function librarian position could not exist as it currently does.

The Libraries embarked on three experiments in an attempt to improve the situation created by the new automation. The first was to bring all technical service processes under one head. The second was to simplify the workflow through the division by reorganizing some the units. The third experiment was with decentralized cataloging.

Decentralized Cataloging

The original plan called for the combination of public services, collection development, database searching and original cataloging duties, all in relation to a specific public service unit. A one-third cataloging, two-thirds public service split was envisioned as the ideal. The librarian would be a full member of the public service division (RISD, Reference and Instructional Services Division) but would keep close ties with the technical services division (BRSD, Bibliographic Resources and Services Division). The dual-function librarians at Penn State are called "adjuncts" or "RISD catalogers."

The cataloging department analysed the volume of original cataloging work created by the rate of acquisition. It was determined that four full-time catalogers or twelve catalogers devoting one-third of their time to cataloging could handle the work load. The perfect opportunity to implement decentralized cataloging presented itself between August 1983 and April 1984 when seven of the ten catalogers at Pattee resigned for a variety of reasons. In April 1984 the position of Humanities/Special Collections Reference and Cataloging Librarian was created. To date this is the only position that has been filled internally. Since 1984 decentralized cataloging has expanded to the Engineering, Physical Sciences, and Life Sciences Libraries as well as a position in the Documents Section. In 1990 two additional librarians were hired, one in the Earth and Mineral Sciences library and the other in the General Reference Section as a business specialist. The original cataloging unit has retained five full-time catalogers.

Decentralized cataloging at Penn State is made possible by the LIAS system. The adjunct catalogers have their own technical service terminals in their public service units. From these terminals the adjuncts can dial up OCLC and RLIN, browse the LC MARC books tapes, and upgrade partial cataloging records previously input by PSU support staff. A particularly powerful feature of LIAS is the SHELF command, which enables the catalogers to establish the appropriateness of new call numbers by browsing existing records in shelf order.

Disadvantages

For every new position there are always some negative aspects. One of the areas that must be addressed is the need to limit the workload of the dual function librarian. Time management becomes an essential tool when having to juggle what comes out to be almost two full time positions. Working in two divisions requires attending twice the number of meetings. Although the flexibility and variety of the job is usually cited as a advantage (increased visibility outside technical services, greater diversity in professional duties, and less chance of "burn-out"), this flexibility can also serve as a drawback. Priority setting becomes very difficult, and there is an inherent conflict of interest: should an item be cataloged following the rules to the letter or should there be a certain degree of flexibility in order to assure optimal patron access?

The most serious problem is that of job retention in regard to training. At Penn State the average "life span" of a dual-function librarian seems to be four to five years. While this might be the average for reference librarians across the board, the problem of training is compounded for dual function positions. The average training period is six months, during which time the librarian works full-time in the Cataloging Department. After the initial formal training period is completed, the schedule is reduced to half-time in cataloging, and then finally to the one-third split. The time devoted to training in cataloging involves a significant investment of staff time and institutional overhead.

There is no one explanation for the turn-over in these positions. Most dual function librarians leave for the same reasons that traditional reference librarians and catalogers leave: jobs with greater administrative and supervisory duties and/or better pay. No follow-up has been done to determine whether or not they leave for more traditional jobs. In spite of the turnover, however, the PSUL administration continues to believe that the time spent in training is a worthwhile investment.

Positive Reactions

When decentralized cataloging was first introduced at Penn State the staff and administration had a number of expectations, the primary hope being that this position would improve the flow of communication between the technical and public service divisions. The cataloger would serve as a liaison and advocate for the public service division. The feeling of the administration is that this expectation has been met. Communication and collaboration between the divisions have greatly improved, making it possible to complete several complex cataloging projects, including the cataloging of maps and local, state, federal, and international documents.

The positive reactions to this position are not limited to the administration alone; other librarians and the support and clerical staff have voiced their approval. No longer is it necessary to go through many layers of supervisors to have a record corrected. Problems of cataloging can be explained and a solution can often be found.

The most important comments come from the split librarians themselves. "I have circumvented the one-dimensional perspective which limits to only one area. I have extended my professional world and experienced personal satisfaction in doing so."[10] "Overall, I thoroughly enjoyed the experience because of the broader scope a split position gives a librarian to understand how a library functions, the needs of users, and how library policy impacts on users."[11]

Having a cataloger in the public service unit is a good use of subject expertise and allows for better understanding of patron needs. The adjuncts have a global perspective on their collections since they participate at every step from initial selection decisions through final disposition of newly cataloged material in the collection. Through daily use of subject heading lists and classification schedules, the adjuncts have a greater in-depth understanding of the structuring of their subject area in the catalog. Finally, their understanding of descriptive cataloging rules enables adjuncts to help patrons retrieve "difficult" material from LIAS, such as conferences, uniform titles, and certain science series.

CONCLUSION

The concept of a dual public-technical services librarian dates back at least to the 1940s, when the University of Nebraska first began considering the divisional plan. For ten or more years the plan seemed successful, but failed to fulfill its initial promise because existing technology could not help the staff cope with increasing workloads. Faced with diminishing university support, the library administration was forced to back away from a non-traditional organization.

At Penn State the dual function position has succeeded for a variety of reasons. Important factors included initial planning in the 1950s for a future integrated library system, willingness to experiment with non-traditional organization, the investment of staff time to recruit and train adjuncts, and the rapid maturing of library technologies throughout the 1970s and 1980s. Automation has given the dual function position a second chance to succeed where it fell short the first time. In spite of turnover among the adjunct catalogers, administrative backing of the positions remains strong, as witnessed by the recent hiring of a documentation and training librarian to provide additional support to the adjuncts. The reorganization of library functional divisions will continue to occupy center stage of library agendas for many years to come.

REFERENCES

1. Frank A. Lundy, Kathryn R. Renfro and Esther M. Shubert, "The Dual Assignment: Cataloging and Reference: A Four-Year Review of Cataloging in the Divisional Plan," Library Resources and Technical Services 3 (1959):176.

2. James G. Neal, "The Evolving Public/Technical Services Relationship: New Opportunities for Staffing the Cataloging Function," in *Recruiting, Educating, and Training Cataloging Librarians*, ed. Sheila S. Intner and Janet Swan Hill (Connecticut: Greenwood Press, 1989), p. 113.

3. Eugene M. Johnson, "Nebraska. University of Nebraska Libraries," in *Encyclopedia of Library and Information Science* v.19 ed. Allen Kent, Harold Lancour and Jay E. Daily (New York: Marcel Dekker, Inc., 1976), p. 223.

4. Frank A. Lundy, "Library Service to Undergraduate College Students," College and Research Libraries 17 (March 1956):145.

5. Kathryn R. Renfro, "Cataloging in the Divisional Library," College and Research Libraries 15 (April 1954):155.

6. Frank A. Lundy, Adapted from "The Divisional Library at Nebraska," Library Journal 80 (June 1955):1303.

7. Eugene M. Johnson, "Nebraska. University of Nebraska Libraries," in *Encyclopedia of Library and Information Science* v.19 ed. Allen Kent, Harold Lancour and Jay E. Daily (New York: Marcel Dekker Inc., 1976), p. 226.

8. Ibid., p. 225.

9. Stuart Forth, "Pennsylvania State University Libraries," in *Encyclopedia of Library and Information Science* v.21 ed. Allen Kent, Harold Lancour and Jay E. Daily (New York: Marcel Dekker Inc., 1976), p. 499.

10. Caroline Blumenthal et al., "Purposeful 'Schizophrenia': Creative Staffing Through the use of Split Positions," *ACRL Conference Proceedings* (Chicago: ACRL, 1989), p. 262-264.

11. Barbara Dean, Personal letter.

RLIN Research Access Project:
An Education in User Expectations

Barbara J. Via

SUMMARY. The increasing availability of computerized information sources and networking capabilities, along with the proliferation of microcomputers in faculty homes and offices, has led to increased demands for direct access to databases. The librarian's role as online search intermediary appears to be changing from performing searches directly to aiding users in doing their own searching. The Research Libraries Information Network (RLIN), one of the major cataloging utilities, offers a wealth of bibliographic information in both its online union catalog, and its many specialized files. The University at Albany Libraries participated in a pilot project involving faculty end-user access to RLIN. This paper reports on the Libraries' experience with the pilot project and the continuing end-user access program for faculty. Despite some reservations about the relative user-friendliness of the RLIN search system, the author enthusiastically endorses the use of RLIN as an end-user database.

INTRODUCTION

Most university campuses have seen over the last three years, a considerable increase in faculty use of microcomputers, resulting in increased faculty interest in direct access to computerized information in the library. The rapid appearance of multiple databases in compact disc format, and the ready availability of computer networks, have raised expectations on the part of at least some faculty members as to the ease with which needed information can be gained. While in years past it was sufficient for the librarian to

Barbara J. Via is Reference Librarian/Bibliographer, University at Albany, SUNY, Thomas E. Dewey Graduate Library for Public Affairs and Policy, Albany, NY 12222.

15

serve as "the keeper of the keys" for computerized files, providing access to files and performing the searches, many faculty are no longer willing to see the librarian as search intermediary. These faculty want the librarian to tell them about available databases, ease their access to these databases, and then leave them to their own devices. The major bibliographic utilities, such as the Research Libraries Information Network (RLIN) and the Online Computer Library Center (OCLC), once considered librarians' tools, searchable only by trained librarians, are now considered by many faculty as merely another computerized source that can aid their research efforts.

RLIN is a national database which serves as a cataloging utility and union catalog for forty-two major research libraries and sixty-three special members (as of September 1991) who belong to the Research Libraries Group (RLG). In addition to serving as a union catalog, RLIN's many computerized files provide a rich resource for scholarly research. The RLIN system is actually comprised of several databases, the largest of which is the online union catalog of members' books and serials, both cataloged and on order. As of December 19, 1990, the database included nearly 38,000,000 book records, and over 3,000,000 serial records. Additionally, the online union catalog includes files of cataloged entries for visual materials, maps, sound recordings, musical scores, archives and manuscripts, and machine-readable datafiles. Over the years, the RLIN system has expanded to include several special databases including the *Avery Index to Architecture Periodicals*, the *Eighteenth Century Short Title Catalog* (ESTC), the *Research in Progress Database* (RIPD), and the recently loaded *Ei Page One*, a citations file covering 3,000 engineering journals and proceedings, among others. The growing body of information available through RLIN makes it a valuable resource for libraries and for scholars.

THE RESEARCH ACCESS PROJECT (PILOT)

For many years, RLIN was considered primarily as a tool for librarians to use for various in-house functions, including cataloging, pre-order searching, and reference. In 1987, however, the Research Libraries Group (RLG) developed a plan to expand its potential user population by providing scholars with direct access to the resources of the RLIN system. In order to test the feasibility of this plan, the Research Access Project was launched in 1988. In implementing the pilot project, RLG hoped to discover, among other things, whether the RLIN system interface could be successfully used by scholars.

LITERATURE REVIEW

Long before this project was launched, articles had appeared in the literature which discussed the use of RLIN as a reference tool. A 1982 article by Farmer discusses RLIN's capabilities as a reference tool and recommends using RLIN to complement searches done on retrieval systems such as BRS, Dialog, and Orbit to quickly verify bibliographic information, to search other libraries' holdings as a union catalog, and to verify interlibrary loans (Farmer, 1982). Flores (1986) discusses the complexities of the RLIN search manual and provides a brief guide, which aims to make RLIN more user-friendly. An especially useful article comparing OCLC, WLN, and RLIN as public service tools provides detailed information on the databases, their indexing, and their search capabilities (Hirst, Thorpe, and Funabiki, 1987). Bruseau (1987) discusses search-only access to the RLIN database as a useful complement to searching other bibliographic utilities. Clever and Dillard (1988) exhort information brokers to consider RLIN as an economical and rich source of information for answering client queries. RLIN's strength as a database for locating United States federal documents is discussed in an article in Government Publications Review. The author reports that at his library, RLIN has become the system of choice for locating federal documents online. He cites RLIN's flexible indexes, and the availability of Boolean operators as particularly useful for government documents searching (Ernest, 1988). Flores and Pritchard (1989) discuss the problems, "both practical and theoretical," with direct-user access to RLIN. They find RLIN to be "unforgiving and generally unfriendly," and suggest that a sub-database be created for end-users that would be more understandable to non-librarians. Richards (1990) discusses the RLIN database and its role in the spectrum of electronic information services available on college and university campuses.

Recently, articles on the RLIN direct access project have begun to appear. Dodson (1988) provides a brief overview of New York University's participation in the pilot project for scholar's access to RLIN. Since Dodson's article was written during the course of the pilot, it does not evaluate the success of the project. An article on an end-user project involving access to RLIN's Avery Index to Architecture Periodicals provides an interesting analysis of that database's particular usefulness as an end-user accessible datafile (Woo, 1988). The value of searching RLIN's special databases for humanists is the focus of a recent article (Muratori, 1990).

IMPLEMENTATION OF THE RLIN ACCESS PROJECT

Eight RLG member libraries, including the University at Albany, agreed to participate in the pilot project which RLG announced in summer of 1987. Over two hundred faculty from the eight institutions signed up for RLIN accounts. Under the terms of this pilot project, special faculty access accounts were to be set up at a rate of $99 for a ten-hour block of search time. Funding, selection of faculty participants, and training were left to the discretion of the individual libraries. At all but one of the participating libraries, faculty accounts were completely subsidized by the host institutions. Offering subsidized accounts seemed a good idea to encourage faculty to give RLIN a try. At Albany, a letter was sent to Deans and Department Chairs from the Director of Libraries, announcing the pilot project and offering library subsidized accounts for up to thirty individuals. The response to this letter yielded the names of twenty-two faculty members willing to sign up for an RLIN account and attend a brief training session.

Eighteen Albany faculty actually followed through and completed a one-hour training session. It became obvious from the training sessions that RLIN was of most interest to faculty from the Social Sciences and Humanities. The Science faculty who had signed up quickly decided that a database that did not offer journal literature citations was of little use to them. Since the library administration had budgeted for thirty faculty accounts, it was decided to carry out a more focused solicitation of faculty by subject bibliographers.

Nine additional faculty agreed to participate in the project as a result of bibliographer contacts. These faculty represented a number of academic disciplines, including French Studies, History, German, and Women's Studies. Each person was provided with a search packet from RLG, which included an RLIN password, instructions for Telenet access, an RLIN searching guide, a list of library identifiers, and an informational brochure about RLIN.

The faculty participants came to the project with varying levels of microcomputer experience. A couple of them had microcomputers but no modem with which to dial out. Others were avid users of micros and were very knowledgeable about computer technology. The faculty members' understanding of what RLIN is, and what kind of information it contains, also varied widely. Faculty who thought that RLIN was a database that includes periodical citations were clearly disappointed, and became disinterested in using their RLIN passwords.

Faculty searchers seemed to find the basic search commands easily understandable. They particularly liked the ability to use Boolean operators in their search statements. The use of the ''also'' command to refine a search to such things as publication date and language was also lauded by faculty. What proved most difficult in training faculty to search RLIN was explaining its use of library jargon. Full MARC records do not lend themselves to easy interpretation by non-librarians. Attempting to explain what a record cluster is, or why a title search turns up matches that in the partial display do not appear to match the entered title, could be frustrating. Another source of frustration was the inability to save search statements. Unlike a search of BRS or Dialog, there are no search statement numbers in RLIN which can be recalled. Thus, once a user has gone on to another search statement, the previous request is lost.

EVALUATION OF THE PROJECT

At the end of the pilot project, the RLG Public Services Committee (PSC) implemented an evaluation of the faculty participants. Among the many issues which the committee hoped to address through a survey of faculty participants were the following:

- Are users willing to pay for direct RLIN access? If so, how much?
- Is the RLIN searching interface a barrier to the use of RLG services?
- What would be the impact of direct RLIN access on the local library, on interlibrary loan, and general awareness of RLG?
- How were participants trained, and were methods and documentation sufficient?
- Was searching easy? and did the searcher consider the use of RLIN a successful experience?

Each local administrator of the project was asked to distribute the evaluation instrument to faculty and collect results for forwarding to the PSC. One hundred and twenty-two faculty completed the evaluation instrument. The evaluation survey provided the PSC with at least partial answers to some of the questions posed above. Forty-five percent of the respondents indicated that they would be willing to pay to search RLIN at a rate listed as $99 for ten hours of connect time. RLIN searches were rated as either "very satisfactory" or "satisfactory" by 91% of the respondents. Seventy-six percent of faculty found using RLIN very easy or easy, while 19% rated using RLIN difficult or very difficult. It is worth noting that although 122 participants completed the evaluation instrument, 23 of them indicated that they had not signed on to RLIN at all after their training session. Furthermore, only 49 participants indicated that they had signed on to RLIN ten or more times during the course of the pilot project. Of 97 responses to a question on frequency of use of interlibrary loan services since having an RLIN account, 19% of the participants indicated that their use of ILL had increased. The answer to this question, and in fact, several of the questions on the survey, rely on participants' subjective responses. There is really no way, from the information gained in the pilot project, to verify whether end-user searching of RLIN has an impact on demand for interlibrary loan services.

Further analysis of the data collected by the PSC is being conducted. Cross-tabulations of data, such as prior computing expertise crossed with the rating of RLIN's ease of use, will provide more meaningful analysis of the faculty's experiences.

Based on observation of faculty use at the University at Albany, and conversations with faculty users, a tentative answer can be given for the RLG Public Service Committee's first question about direct access: is the search interface a barrier to direct access? There is no doubt that the RLIN search interface is somewhat of a barrier to *successful* end-user searching. The basic search commands are simple, but unsuccessful searches do not yield any meaningful response from the system as to the incorrectness of the search statement. Thus, the unsuspecting user can receive a zero result to his query, without realizing that the search statement was incorrectly input. The inability to save search steps and combine them is certainly another barrier to successful searching. However, despite its flaws, faculty report that the search system is usable, and generally, they do not find it burdensome to learn.

FACULTY ACCESS BEYOND THE PILOT PROJECT

During the period of the pilot project, faculty participants at Albany came and went. With monthly invoices from RLG showing each account's use, it became clear that some accounts were being very actively used, while many others were sitting completely idle. When the pilot project was drawing to a close, in Spring 1989, RLG began to promote end-user searching more directly to scholars, and announced the ability to search RLIN files via Internet, a government sponsored computer network that links universities and research centers across the country. At the University at Albany, it was decided that for the next year, at least, the Library would continue to subsidize faculty search costs and promote faculty end-user searching of the RLIN system via Internet. In the Fall of 1989, a letter was sent to the Dean of the College of Humanities and Fine Arts, advising faculty of the availability of RLIN search accounts. A brief article on RLIN was also included in the Library's external newsletter. As of fall 1990, the University at Albany has 26 faculty with RLIN accounts. A few of these faculty were participants in the pilot project, but many are new searchers. This latest group of faculty searchers includes some who are very active and enthusiastic RLIN users. For these account holders, RLIN provides an essential component of their research efforts.

INTERVIEWS WITH FACULTY

The author recently interviewed three of the faculty searchers in order to gauge the value that they place on access to RLIN for their research, and their views on its user-friendliness. Dr. Gerald Zahavi, a professor of history who teaches courses in local and regional history and quantitative methods in history, has used RLIN to a great extent, both for his own research and as a teaching tool for students in his local history course. His particular interest in the RLIN database is in the area of local and regional history, especially New York State archives. He searches RLIN for both known items and topics. He makes particular use of the Archives and Manuscripts Control (AMC) file. Dr. Zahavi finds the basic search keys easy to use and the results are very satisfactory. He has some reservations about the title word search because if the word searched is too common, the searcher can get stuck waiting a long time for the system to respond. He suggests there should be a simple means to abort the search statement after one has put in a too-common word. Dr. Zahavi reports that his use of interlibrary loan services has definitely increased as a result of his ability to search the RLIN files. He finds the RLIN datafiles invaluable for searching for manuscript collections for New York State counties, since the holdings of all New York State repositories are available through AMC. He also finds RLIN very useful for compiling bibliographies for himself and his students. Dr. Zahavi states that by having RLIN available for personal searching, he does not feel the lack of collections locally, since through RLIN he has access to millions and millions of volumes in libraries across the country.

Dr. Charles Hartman, Chair of the Chinese Studies Department at Albany, has also found RLIN an exceptional aid to his research efforts. He uses the system for known-item verification and topical searching almost equally. Like Dr. Zahavi, Dr. Hartman reports a definite increase in his use of interlibrary loan service since obtaining an RLIN account. Since he is often looking for an exact edition of an old Chinese book, he finds RLIN very useful for verifying bibliographic information. With this information in hand, he then can go to the interlibrary loan office with a printed citation to the exact edition he seeks. Dr. Hartman states that RLIN greatly speeds up his research, and saves him an enormous amount of time and expense. Equipped with his printed results from an RLIN search, he can visit RLG libraries and go right to the material he needs. Dr. Hartman hopes to see the records of more of the largest collections of rare Chinese books included in RLIN in the future.

A professor in the School of Information Science and Policy, Dr. Millicent Lenz has used RLIN extensively both during the pilot project, and this past year. Dr. Lenz uses RLIN most frequently for known-item searches. She finds the system user-friendly and retrieves expected results from her searches. She recently published a book that was heavily documented, and found that RLIN was extremely valuable for verifying items in her bibliography and footnotes. She finds the RLIN response time very good, and describes RLIN as a positive component of her research efforts.

IMPROVEMENTS TO END-USER SEARCHING

As a result of the pilot project, RLG has begun to improve the user interface in order to make it more easily searched by non-librarians. An RLG press release, dated March 1990, announced the addition of subject word search access. This is a valuable enhancement since the end-user no longer has to know the exact Library of Congress subject heading in order to search by topic. Other enhancements to the system include expanded hours of access, on-screen prompts for next command, help commands, and the ability to download records to disk or printer continuously. With the newly introduced "help" commands, the user can now type in help anywhere in his searching and retrieve screens of information on searching RLIN successfully. The user can ask the system to explain the also command while in the help mode. The retrieved response is an introductory screenful of information on the use of the also command, along with further help options to choose from at the bottom of the screen. A new searching flip-chart, produced by RLG, is an excellent aid for novice and experienced searchers alike.

Although recently announced changes in the RLIN end-user interface are welcome, more needs to be done if RLG hopes to successfully market RLIN directly to scholars as a fee-based service. There need to be many more help commands in the end-user interface. A detailed description of all of the special files should be searchable online. RLG would be wise to study the search interfaces offered by some of the major online database vendors and implement some of the better features of their systems, such as use of adjacency operators, and the ability to save search statements and combine them. The ability to search parts of a title phrase not found at the beginning of the title would be a useful enhancement.

The introduction of OCLC's new search system, EPIC, brings a tough competitor into the market for end-user access to large union catalog databases. OCLC obviously spent considerable time and money developing a very sophisticated search system. The EPIC system has many of the same features as the foremost online database vendors. The searching capabilities allow for considerable flexibility of search options. Proximity operators can be used to specify that search terms are within a specified number of words of each other. Indexes can be scanned and an alphabetical list of index entries, with number of records for each term will be displayed. Search statements can be saved and search results can be sorted and sub-sorted. Scholars will undoubtedly want accounts for searching EPIC from their own computers. An impediment to offering EPIC accounts to scholars is the cost. There is a connect hour rate (recently reduced from $37 to $24/connect hour) as well as citation charges for displaying certain record formats. An advantage of providing end-user access to RLIN, for member institutions of RLG, is that it is not very expensive to provide access to RLIN. At the University at Albany, a very large block of searches is paid for each year, and faculty searches are simply deducted from the same prepaid block of searches which librarians use in their work.

CONCLUSION

The pilot project did not fully answer the questions about end-user searching posed by RLG. Although it provided some information on the user-friendliness of the search interface, it did not provide any real data on the impact of end-user searching on interlibrary loan. Although some faculty report that their use of ILL has increased as a result of having RLIN accounts, this has not been verified by the interlibrary loan librarian at the University at Albany. It is obvious that the faculty searchers are more aware of RLG's existence and purpose than before they had accounts. However, it is really not possible, with the data collected thus far, to determine whether faculty account holders are searching RLIN successfully. As with all end-user searching, one suspects that if the searcher finds something, he or she will feel that the search is successful.

The experience of faculty searching of the RLIN database at the University at Albany has been a positive one. The benefits of direct access to RLIN are slowly being recognized by scholars. It is too early to tell if the role of librarians as information gatekeepers will be seriously impacted by scholars having direct access to such services as RLIN. At the present time, the actual number of account holders is low when put in perspective of actual faculty on campus (there are currently twenty-six active accounts, about fifteen of which receive frequent use). Librarians play an instructional role with RLIN searchers in training new users, and keeping account holders abreast of searching enhancements. Although it is possible, even now, for a faculty member to obtain an RLIN account directly from RLG, bypassing the Library completely, it seems that there will continue to be a vital role for librarians in facilitating access to RLIN and other online files, training end-users, and facilitating the procurement of materials identified through online searching.

REFERENCES

Bruseau, Larry. "Search-Only Access to the RLIN Database," PNLA Quarterly 51 (Spring 1987):9-13.

Clever, Elaine Cox and David P. Dillard. "RLIN: a Databank to Consider," Online 12 (May 1988):28-29.

Dodson, Melanie. "Faculty Access to RLIN at New York University:RLG's Research Access Project," College & Research Libraries News 49 (September 1988): 522-523.

Ernest, Douglas J. "Accessing federal government publications with RLIN," Government Publications Review 15 (1988):237-244.

Farmer, Sharon Cline. "RLIN as a Reference Tool," Online 6 (September 1982): 14-22.

Flores, Arturo A. and Teresa N. Pritchard. "End-user Access to Bibliographic Databases; Or, Happy Trails: Public Users Ride High in the RLIN Saddle," Legal Reference Services Quarterly 9 (1989):165-173.

Flores, Arturo A. "A User Friendly Guide to RLIN for Friendly Users," Legal Reference Services Quarterly 5 (Winter 1985/86):43-53.

Hirst, Donna L., Suzanne Thorpe, and Ruth Patterson Funabiki. "A Comparison of OCLC, WLN, and RLIN for Public Services: A 1985 Update," Legal Reference Services Quarterly 6 (Fall/Winter 1986):141-158.

Muratori, Fred. "RLIN Special Databases: Serving the Humanist," *Database, 13 (Oct. 1990):48-52.*

Richards, David. "The Research Libraries Group," in Campus Strategies for Libraries and Electronic Information, Digital Press, 1990, 57-75.

Woo, Janice. "The Online Avery Index End-User Pilot Project: Final Report," Information Technology & Libraries 7 (September 1988):223-229.

How Did We Get Here: Thoughts on the Convergence of Reference and Technical Services

Ree DeDonato

SUMMARY. The convergence of reference and technical services has developed as a result of the impact of technology on libraries. With new abilities to enhance and expand services, librarians increasingly turned their focus from separate departmental projects to wider ranging access services. The trend toward Access Services is reinforcing a shared commitment to service and is encouraging stronger interdepartmental working relationships.

No one would deny that ACCESS is the key buzzword in libraries today. The definition of ACCESS often varies. In the literature and in discussions, we speak of bibliographic access, information access, physical access, remote access, direct access and more lately Access Services. A common thread among all of these types of access is the idea of connecting: a description to an item; a question to an answer; a user to a source, and so on. Emphasizing access instead of, say, reference or cataloging might be fairly new, but its connotation of linking, facilitating, bringing together, has been embedded in the business of libraries for a long time.

Reference librarians have always been concerned with listening to questions and interpreting them in order to guide users through a web of sources and information. The librarian's expertise in use of the library's collections and understanding of the subject matter facilitates the growth of the user's knowledge. Catalogers have devised ways of describing individual "packages" of information

Ree DeDonato is Head, General and Humanities Reference, Bobst Library, New York University, 70 Washington Square South, New York, NY 10012.

27

(e.g., books, serials) in such a way as to bring some organizing principle to bear so related items would be brought together for the ease of the user. The means — whether that be reference assistance or bibliographic description — are different indeed but the end is the same, the making of a connection between the seeker and the sought.

If providing access or facilitating connections have always been part of our professional responsibility, why does "Access Services" seem like such a revolutionary concept? Is it just a new name for the same functions or is it the representation of something substantively different in the way libraries are operating? Perhaps the following comments will suggest a few answers to this question from the perspective of an academic reference librarian who also happens to be a middle-manager, department head, subject bibliographer and a library user as well.

TECHNOLOGY AS A CATALYST FOR CHANGE

Technology has been a major catalyst for change in our institutions. A recent article in *The Journal of Academic Librarianship* discusses how technology has changed reference librarianship. One of the first points made is that technological innovation requires an institutional change in order to assure the most effective use of the new technology.[1] The convergence of reference and technical services is one of the ways our institutions are changing in response to technology. Automation has enabled libraries to enhance, expand and link operations to both deliver better services and make them more convenient for users and staff. Public and technical components of library operations are converging as we emphasize the primary goal of access.

In today's academic library one would be hard pressed in looking at services to mark where the "technical" ends and the "public" begins. At NYU's Bobst Library, for instance, there are computer workstations in reference centers to access local and remote databases. There are acquisitions and cataloging staff working at the public catalog information desk. Previously restricted components of our online system are made available on public services staff terminals. Reference staff are on planning committees for the continued development of various automation projects. E-mail, word processing, FAX, downloading to pc's, are all a routine part of everyone's work.

Initially, it seemed that public service departments were on the receiving end of library automation. As such, we were rarely an integral part of the planning and development stages of library automation projects. Public services staff were brought in during the testing stage to stand in as users on the premise that if they could deal with automated circulation or online catalogs, then the public should be able to as well. If a template for recording reference statistics was needed or a quick logon procedure for dial-out services, they were developed and installed "ready made." The reference librarian's understanding of these processes was not considered essential. But as the pace and scope of automation projects increased, public services staff became more involved in planning, developing and creating. Technology was no longer something which existed "behind the scenes"; it became part of many very visible and heavily used services. The reference librarians were forced to take responsibility for and claim ownership of the systems they were using. Task forces were formed with members from different library units to create online catalog help screens, to design interfaces, to instruct one another in the use of various systems, to write documentation and user guides. This working partnership brought about the development of a new concept in library functionality — access services.

ACCESS SERVICES/STAFF PERSPECTIVES

With public and technical services working together more closely, all librarians came to share a kind of global thinking about the mission of libraries. All of our jobs are concerned with providing access; it is not the domain of any one functional group. Although librarians are and probably will continue to specialize in particular functional areas of librarianship (e.g., systems, reference, circulation, collection development), our separate functions are interacting with greater frequency. We combine areas of expertise and link separate operations to one another to provide better library service. Even in libraries which do not have a designated unit named "access services,'' thinking in terms of access and not just in terms of reference or technical services strengthens the working relationship among different library departments.

Global thinking is another change which is part of the trend toward Access Services. When specific library activities, staff and departments are reorganized into a unit called Access Services, this global thinking is translated into something tangible. Scanning the position announcements in *American Libraries*, *C&RL News*, or the *Chronicle of Higher Education* gives us some examples of what kinds of departments and services are being joined to form the new Access Services units. A common grouping includes a mix of circulation, reserves, interlibrary loan and stack maintenance, with the occasional addition of copy services, branch libraries, library privileges, and microforms. These are logical groupings of departments which have similar functions. We should develop, however, new configurations of interdepartmental cooperation to truly implement the global meaning of providing access.

One example might be end-user searching in an academic library as a likely activity for an Access Services unit. End-user search services are usually reference department projects because the databases involved often represent a variant form of something already in the reference collection. Reference staff know the intellectual content of the database and the use patterns of the existing print collection so they will initiate the selection of the database(s). Database services unit staff might help evaluate the searching software or vendor support. Systems staff might then be called upon to assist with the installation of necessary hardware and software. Then bibliographic access to these machine-readable files might be requested of cataloging staff so users will be able to find them in the same way that they find the print sources. Finally, user training might be developed by bibliographic instruction staff or by a task force comprised of other members of the reference department.

Another example of an increasingly important type of access service is document delivery. Interlibrary Loan has been performing this service for years. However, the current growth of document delivery services in libraries goes beyond ILL's traditional library-to-library delivery route. Those of us within RLG (the Research Libraries Group), for instance, are eagerly awaiting the full development and testing of the Document Transmission Workstation (DTW) for use with RLG's RLIN (Research Libraries Information Network) system. The DTW can scan, store, transmit documents to other workstations and print them out with higher resolution and at less cost than most current fax machines.[2]

The presumption is that with the DTW in place, a faculty member or student will be able to identify relevant research by first searching RLIN and then sending a request for the item from his or her own PC which will be transmitted to the library's RLG DTW. From there, the request goes on through RLIN's ILL subsystem to another RLG library which owns the item. This source library will then scan the item into its DTW for direct transmission back to the original requestor, while storing the scanned item in a central electronic database which may be queried by others to satisfy future requests. The connections between the libraries and the user are very strong, even though the complex document delivery process is somewhat invisible to the user.

Until the DTW is ready, RLG has already begun to enhance its document delivery capability by the inclusion of the new Citations (CIT) File in RLIN. [3] CIT contains Engineering Information (Ei) Inc.'s *Ei Page One* database of over 600,000 citations covering some 3,000 journals and conference proceedings in engineering fields, from January 1986 to the present. RLIN users, either librarians or end users with personal access RLIN accounts, can search this file as they would any of the other RLIN bibliographic files. Fulltext articles may be requested by phone, FAX or online through the RLIN ILL subsystem. The user has the option to have the library continue to serve as the intermediary supplier of the material (if requested via ILL) or the user can go directly to Ei. In either case, users have much greater flexibility and control of the process than they had before, yet the library is still part of the access chain.

The development of these kinds of innovative library services will continue to require strong links between technical and public service functions. End-user searching and document delivery are just two examples of what "access services" might become. As other library initiatives are developed, the need for combined expertise and interdepartmental planning will be strengthened. Access services will continue to promote the convergence of reference and technical services.

ACCESS SERVICES/PATRON PERSPECTIVES

We understand that our individual contributions are more firmly tied to the goal of providing all-round access. At the same time, the development of new access services may be influencing library users to expand their own thinking about library services, as well as raising their expectations. If all these end-user search services can make it so easy to come up with a list of 30 references on the desired topic, why doesn't the library have them for every subject area possible, and why can't they all be full text, not just citations and sometimes abstracts? Why aren't they just part of the online catalog anyway so everything is in one place and works the same? Remember how last time you found this for me at a library in California and had it faxed here right away? Can you do that again for this new PhD thesis I heard was just completed? Can't we just get printouts of everything without having to go to the stacks to look for the journals and books? And by the way, if computers make using this information so easy and quick, why is it taking so long for the library's online catalog to include everything in the library and not just material from the last 10 to 15 years?

This barrage of questions is familiar to all of us working at reference desks because every day our users ask them with greater and greater frequency. The kind of access services we are providing are making them more keenly aware that libraries can provide more than "just books." How realistic the demands for service are may vary with the user's level of sophistication, but the idea that the library can bring things together to extend its resources, save time and make things easier is catching on among all types of users.

The fact that we are able to provide more for our users is a positive thing. The fact that users see the library as a more dynamic place and want to take advantage of what it has to offer is also positive. Libraries are becoming a kind of "one stop shopping" information mart to users: drop-in or dial-in; look it up; print it out; download it; if it's not local, get it by FAX, mail, whatever. One cause for concern, however, is that a "one stop shopping" attitude among users starts to make everything seem easy, including the part where they have to put critical thinking skills to work. Users have to develop their "computer logic" so they will understand the contents of databases and construct meaningful searches. They have to exercise good judgment about what to use from the long list of citations which a computer search produces in just a few minutes. They have to think about the authority of the information retrieved and not accept it at face value. They have to focus on which information resource they are choosing and not make their selections only on the basis of speed and ease of use. Users still have to know something about what they want in order to use the library most effectively, and librarians are needed to help them develop these skills and to sift through the vast array of information now accessed. "Access to excess" is what users will have if we lose sight of our role.[4]

CHANGES IN JOB DESCRIPTIONS

Another result of the convergence of reference and technical services is the changing nature of our job responsibilities. Reference librarians have to be more technologically literate and technical services librarians have to be more people oriented in order to work effectively in today's library environment. Today, the job of an administrator, subject selector or reference librarian cannot be done without both understanding and using the technology at one's disposal. Nor could any of these jobs remain viable without an institution's continued commitment to implementing technologically based enhancements in the library. Most librarians would agree that without technology there would not be enough hours in the day to be involved in the many projects which we consider part of our day-to-day work. How could we seek advice, and get it within minutes, from colleagues across the country, without electronic mail or FAX? How could we handle the numerous, complex reference questions fielded every day without being able to draw upon online or CD-ROM databases, library catalogs and major bibliographic utilities? How could we document our services and communicate our needs to library administration, create point-of-use signage and user guides in a timely fashion without the use of word processing and statistical software packages? How could we evaluate and build our collections without browsing through online catalogs or doing a few quick citation searches to keep abreast of newly published research?

WHAT HAS TECHNOLOGY DONE FOR US?

Technology has not necessarily saved us time, but it has made us more productive. It has not made things simple, but it has allowed us to do complex things more easily. In public services we are juggling more projects and are involved in a greater variety of activities all the time. From where we are now, it is hard to imagine that it could be any other way. "Technostress"[5] is a condition we deal with as routinely as we might deal with shrinking budgets or staff turnover. Along with colleagues in technical services, it seems we move back and forth between coping with and controlling our library environment.

During the most recent annual ALA Conference, a number of programs addressed the expansion of job responsibilities in different ways. The RASD (Reference and Adult Services Division) Management of Reference Services Committee and its CODES (Collection Development & Evaluation Section) Dual Assignments Discussion Group co-sponsored a panel/discussion program entitled "Divided Loyalties or Common Ground: Managing Professionals with Multiple Reporting Lines or Functions."[6] The focus of the program was both on effective management strategies for dealing with expanded responsibilities and on evaluating whether multiple assignments lead to job enrichment or fragmentation. The comments of panelists and members of the audience indicated clearly that for reference librarians, there is indeed a shift toward increased functional responsibilities. This shift has contributed to the changes in the role of the reference librarian. Instead of concentrating on direct public assistance, the job may also include collection development, online searching, circulation and bibliographic instruction. It seems that librarians' individual roles are crossing functional lines just as individual projects are being developed by coordinated efforts from different library departments. The lines of distinction between job descriptions and the organizational hierarchies are blurring as services expand.

WHERE ARE WE GOING?

Where the convergence of reference and technical services will ultimately lead us is not yet clear. So far, we have strengthened our shared understanding of the commitment to facilitate access. There has been a greater appreciation for each other's expertise and skills. A closer working relationship has been developed among various library units as services have been extended and improved. Users' expectations of the library are increasing although their perception of how to use its resources still seems oversimplified. The process of convergence has not been a deliberate one; rather it grew out of the impact of technology on libraries and its influence on expanding services. As technology continues to infuse our workplace, it will be imperative that we keep learning new skills and that we keep working together to bring further innovations to library services.

REFERENCES

1. Clark N. Hallman, "Technology: Trigger for Change in Reference Librarianship," *Journal of Academic Librarianship* 16 (1990): 204.

2. "RLG's Innovative New Document Transmission Workstation Outfaxes the FAX," *RLG Press Release*, November 2, 1990.

3. "RLIN Offers Ei Engineering Citations and Document Delivery," *RLG Press Release*, October 22, 1990.

4. "Access to Excess? Issues of the Information Explosion," Annual Symposium of ACRL/NY, the Greater NY Metropolitan Area Chapter of the Association of College & Research Libraries, November 14, 1990.

5. Lynn C. Hattendorf, "Reference Services" in *ALA Yearbook of Library and Information Services '90* 15 (1990): 208.

6. *Information Access—Back to the Basics*, 109th Annual Conference, American Library Association, Chicago, June 23-28, 1990.

Access vs. Ownership:
Changing Roles for Librarians

David Tyckoson

SUMMARY. Throughout the entire history of libraries, the primary objective of any library has been to collect and house information of interest to the specific clientele which it serves. Libraries operated under the premise that materials would be obtained by the library for use on site by those persons authorized to have access to that information. As we move towards the twenty-first century, this concept of the primary function of the library must be questioned. Due to several factors, the library can no longer function solely as a warehouse of information. In order to survive as information professionals for the future, librarians must shift their emphasis from one based on ownership to one based on access. This paper will examine the factors behind the need for such changes and will also examine their impact on the role of the librarian as an information professional.

BACKGROUND

The two paradigms of access and ownership can and do produce conflict within libraries. We are currently experiencing a schizophrenic period in library development, where our patrons view the library with one set of expectations and we view ourselves with a somewhat different set. Patrons tend to view the library as information providers; we tend to view ourselves as information collectors. Although access and ownership are not mutually incompatible, they do produce different sets of criteria for measuring the success and failure of the library. Several studies have been done on the differences and conflict between public and technical services.[1] These

---

David Tyckoson is Head of Reference at University of Albany, SUNY, Albany, NY 12222.

studies have emphasized the effects of library automation, changing job functions, and misperceptions between the two divisions. Many of these problems may be directly traced to the conflict between the two different paradigms in which they operate.

Public services librarians are the members of the library community who have most embraced the paradigm of access. This shift in thinking among those who interact with the public is probably not in response to some great forward-thinking vision inherent in public services, but is a result of a survival tactic created in response to patron demands. Although many reference questions concern information owned by the library, an ever growing number of questions are answered by materials outside of the home library's collection. This fact is mirrored in the growth in the use of interlibrary loan, which can be used as a measure of the number of information requests filled by sources external to the originating library collection. For example, among ARL libraries interlibrary loan traffic has risen from an average of 14,206 transactions per library in 1974 to 23,999 transactions in 1989.[2] This growth has occurred despite many of the problems associated with interlibrary loan, including the notoriously slow delivery of materials. With new technologies that promise more rapid information retrieval and delivery, such as electronic data communications and telefacsimile, this trend can only continue. Surveys of patrons indicate that "they do not want to listen to a litany of possible delays; they want quick and reliable delivery of materials".[3] This same statement could be made in regards to reference questions; patrons do not want to hear why the source is not in the library's collection — they only want the answer to their question. Patron attitudes have greatly influenced the nature of reference service, causing it to shift from answering factual questions contained in reference books to identifying and retrieving information sources regardless of their physical location. Patron interaction has forced reference librarians to at least partially adopt the paradigm of access.

While librarians in public services have confronted the paradigm of access, other divisions of the library still operate primarily under the paradigm of ownership. Collection development is based almost entirely on the acquisition of materials to be added to the collection. The systems of collection development that were developed in the nineteenth century are still functioning intact in the 1990s. In most libraries, the greater part of the materials budget is used to subscribe to serials or to purchase individual monographs and very little funding is allocated for resource sharing. Recent ARL statistics demonstrate the magnitude of the commitment to the paradigm of ownership. Out of an average acquisitions budget of $3,083,287 for ARL libraries in 1986, 97% was allocated for the direct purchase of materials for the library collection. Only 3% of the average budget was spent on other materials, including access to online vendors and bibliographic utilities. It is clear from these figures that ownership still dominates most academic collection development.

For technical services librarians, the paradigm of ownership dominates every aspect of the activities. In nearly every library in the country, the acquisitions department (or its equivalent) purchases materials to be owned in the library's collection, the serials department checks in serials owned by the library, the physical processing department prepares items for storage in the collection, and the cataloging department indexes and organizes the materials obtained for the collection. The primary role of a Technical Services Division is to obtain, organize, and index the materials included in the library collection. Technical Services as an organizational function was developed to effectively and efficiently process materials obtained for the library collection and, until now, there has been little opportunity to deal with information not owned by the parent institution.

While traditional technical services departments perform very well in organizing material within the library, the automation efforts of the last twenty years have illustrated some of the problems of a technical services function limited to owned materials. The catalog, which is one of the primary products of technical services, is more a finding tool than a source of information. This has become much more obvious as more and more libraries develop online public access catalogs. Patron expectations for the catalog are frequently not met. The addition of bibliographic databases such as ERIC and MEDLINE to the OPAC represents the first step in expanding into the era of access. As more and more libraries begin to offer access to information outside the library through their catalogs, technical services librarians will gradually become more involved with indexing and describing information not owned by the library. However, at present very few libraries have even taken the risk of indexing the special collections of materials within their collection, such as government publications, microform sets, or technical reports. Although users expect the catalog to provide them with information of all types regardless of its location, most library catalogs today are merely indexes to the book collection owned by the particular library.

LIBRARIAN ROLES FOR THE FUTURE

The two paradigms come into conflict when they result in different expectations of what type of information the library should provide, which services the library should offer, and how resources should be allocated to support those services. Many of the differences that we see between collection development, public services, and technical services may be directly attributed to the fact that these three traditional divisions of library operations are at times operating from different perspectives. Technical services librarians require resources to effectively describe and index library collections. Collection development librarians require resources to both purchase materials for the library collection and to obtain access to materials outside the collection. And public services librarians require resources to identify and locate materials for library users both inside and outside the primary library collection. Each of these objectives is an important aspect of library service, but all three cannot be met with current limited resources. As we move from the paradigm of ownership to the paradigm of access, librarians in each of the three divisions will be required to think and act in different ways.

For public services librarians, the primary change will be an increased emphasis on document delivery. Library patrons are not concerned about the ultimate origin of the information that they receive, only that it be available within a reasonable period of time following its request. Public services librarians must become skilled not only at retrieving information from within their own library's collection, but also from sources external to the library. Public services librarians will need to become familiar with indexing services and document delivery services that may be located anywhere in the world. They must become as knowledgeable about communications methods and search procedures of remote databases as they are about the catalogs and reference materials of their own institutions. Public services librarians must also play a key role in teaching users how to obtain access to information. In public services, a change in paradigm has already begun to take effect in each of these areas. Barring any significant changes in library budgets, the pace of this shift will only accelerate over the next decade.

For collection development librarians, a shift in paradigm implies a far greater change in the way that the division functions. The current method of selecting and ordering materials is directly tied to the concept that those materials will become part of the library collection. With a shift to the paradigm of access, collection development librarians will need to allocate significantly more resources for materials that may not become part of the library collection. This adds an even greater sense of uncertainty to what has never been an exact science. Whereas in the past libraries decided to either acquire or not to acquire an item, collection development librarians of the future will need to select among several different levels of access to information. Those materials that are in the highest demand by the patrons of the library will still most likely be purchased for the collection. Ownership thus becomes a subset of access, with the information in the library collection available immediately upon request. For materials that are in moderate demand, libraries will purchase access to the information but will not purchase the information itself. In this case, the material is not contained in the collection but can be retrieved in a short time when needed. For those materials in low demand, libraries will order the information as needed. And finally, for materials not in demand, the library will decide to neither own nor access those items.

In order to achieve this four-tiered hierarchy of information access, libraries must re-examine their processes for acquiring information. More funds must be allocated for accessing materials which the library will not necessarily own. Many libraries have already begun to move in this direction with the establishment of deposit accounts with organizations such as the National Technical Information Service, Government Printing Office, or University Microfilms. In these cases, a library will estimate the demand of its users on these sources and allocate funds accordingly. Although some works will be purchased from each of these vendors, the library does not know in advance precisely which works to obtain until it receives input from its patrons. In such a situation, the library has set aside funding to access materials from these vendors, rather than attempting to purchase all necessary materials in advance.

Another example of purchasing access to information is the allocation of funds for searching databases provided by online vendors such as BRS and Dialog. In this case, the library allocates certain funds to be spent for this purpose and then purchases exactly the information that the patron needs at the time that it is requested. The "fee vs. free" debate of the late 1970s may be viewed as one of the first public acknowledgements of the ownership vs. access problem. Library administrators, who had operated primarily in the ownership mode, were very reluctant to allocate funds for a service that would put an unknown and potentially unlimited drain on the materials budget. However, online searchers, who were operating in the mode of providing access to library patrons, argued that online services should be provided free to their patrons just like other library services. While newer technologies such as CD-ROM and the loading of databases into online public access catalogs have reduced our reliance on online vendors, this form of access is one that will continue to be used for information in relatively low demand.

Finally, collection development librarians have begun to move into the area of access through cooperative collection development activities. Driven primarily by funding rather than philosophy, the relative decline in library budgets with respect to publications output has forced some libraries to examine new ways of obtaining information. The most popular coordinated collection development programs divide publications by subject area among several libraries, with the provision that users of one participating library will be able to obtain the materials contained in any of the others. Although still based primarily on the concept of ownership, the ownership becomes collective rather than individual. Yet even this type of access has grown very slowly. As late as 1971, only a very few libraries were engaged in any cooperative collection development activities.[4] Although participation has grown significantly during the last two decades, especially in areas where strong library systems have developed, funding for networking in the typical library is still only a very small fraction of the overall materials budget.

The philosophy of library service adopted by collection development librarians will drive the direction of libraries in the twenty-first century. If libraries continue to collect materials under the paradigm of ownership, they will be increasingly unable to serve a broad public and will be forced to narrow their focus and scope. Unless the economics of information change significantly, libraries operating under this philosophy may be forced to return to the days when they served only a small, well-defined clientele. If this is the case, the next century may see a return to the private libraries of the past. However, a change in philosophy to one based on access will allow libraries to continue to serve the information needs of a broad public. The library based on access will evolve into something that will look very different from the library of today, consisting primarily of indexes to information (in both print and electronic forms) rather than the information itself. In many ways, the academic and public libraries of the future may well resemble the special libraries of today.

For technical services librarians, a change to the paradigm of access will require a total re-evaluation of the functions that they provide. Although advances in technical services have made this area of the library the most automated of any of the three divisions, technical services librarians are generally using that automation to expedite the ownership of materials. The automation of technical services has been used to build large, highly accurate databases of the information purchased by the library. Unfortunately, these databases are increasingly failing to meet the demands of our patrons. This failure is not due to any inaccuracy of the information contained in the database, but by the lack of the types of information patrons expect the database to contain.[5] As libraries move from an era of ownership to one of access, the primary role of technical services librarians will continue to be as database managers. However, the databases managed will consist primarily of materials not owned within the library's internal collection. The biggest challenge to technical services in the next century will not be to organize information within the library under a single set of cataloging rules, but to integrate large amounts of information into the catalog from a wide array of diverse sources. A related function of technical services librarians will be data communications management, linking databases of one library with those of other information providers. Technical services librarians will be responsible for establishing the networks through which patrons identify and retrieve information. In this respect, they will be performing tasks that are frequently a part of public services today.

CONCLUSIONS

Only time will tell if the paradigm of access is to replace the paradigm of ownership. The concept of ownership is deeply embedded in all that we do in libraries. It will take a dramatic change in mindset to supplant this idea. Two thousand years of library tradition will not be replaced in a decade or even in a century. Not all libraries will change their operations from one based on ownership to one based on access. Those that continue to work under the paradigm of ownership will be required to collect in narrower and narrower fields serving smaller groups of patrons. Libraries based on ownership may return to the model of the private libraries of the past. Those libraries that wish to serve a wider public will be forced to adopt the paradigm of access if they also wish to remain as viable information centers. If libraries will not provide access to information, our patrons will obtain that access elsewhere.

REFERENCES

1. Some recent articles on the public services/technical services conflict include: Altmann, Anne E. "The Academic Library of Tomorrow: Who will Do What?" Canadian Library Journal, v. 45, June 1988, pp. 147-152; Bishoff, Liz. "Technical Services/Public Services Cooperation: What's Next?" Technical Services Quarterly, v. 6, 1989, pp. 23-27; Cargill, Jennifer. "Integrating Public and Technical Services Staffs to Implement the New Mission of Libraries." Journal of Library Administration, v. 10, 1989, pp. 21-31; Intner, Sheila S. "The Technical Services Mystique." Technicalities, v. 7, January 1987, pp. 8-11; and McCombs, Gillian. "Public and Technical Services: Disappearing Barriers." Wilson Library Bulletin, v. 61, November 1986, pp. 25-28.

2. Association of Research Libraries. Academic Library Statistics. Washington, D.C.: The Association, Annual. Data for this study was taken from the 1973-1974, 1986-1987, and 1988-1989 reports.

3. Ford, Barbara and Paul A. Frisch. "Interlibrary Loan: A Window on the Information World?" in Fennell, Janice C. Building on the First Century: Proceedings of the Fifth National Conference of the Association of College and Research Libraries. Chicago: Association of College and Research Libraries, 1989, pp. 319-322.

4. See Part A, Table 4, "Library Services Provided from Outside This Library," and Part B, Table 4, "Participate in Cooperative Acquisition," for a list of libraries engaged in these activities. Data is taken from: U.S. Department of Education. National Center for Educational Statistics. Library Statistics of Colleges and Universities. Washington, D.C.: Government Printing Office, 1971.

5. Tyckoson, David A. "The 98% Solution: The Failure of the Catalog and the Role of Electronic Databases." Technicalities, v. 9, February 1989, pp. 8-12.

II. TECHNICAL SERVICES PERSPECTIVE

The Blurring of Divisional Lines Between Technical and Public Services: An Emphasis on Access

Sara Evans Davenport

SUMMARY. Penfield Library at the State University of New York College at Oswego has for many years maintained a strong commitment towards providing access to information. The traditional division between technical services and public services was de-emphasized beginning in the early 1970s, and the lines between those two divisions continue to become less and less defined. All librarians now provide reference service and are trained in basic technical services operations. This policy, which is supported by a variety of cross-training activities, enhances access to materials for library patrons and benefits library staff through supporting the freedom to pursue a variety of professional interests.

Penfield Library at the State University of New York College at Oswego has for many years maintained a strong commitment towards patron service and faculty and student research. This com-

Sara Evans Davenport is Head of Serials and Acquisitions Penfield Library, State University of New York College at Oswego, Oswego, NY 13126-3514.

mitment has allowed the creation of an environment in which library staff can enjoy their work and still maintain a primary emphasis on high quality user service. The traditional division of staff support between technical services and public services was de-emphasized beginning in the early 1970s, and the lines between those two divisions continue to become less and less defined. Before describing Penfield's efforts towards a productive use of library staff for the benefit of library patrons, an explanation of the college and library environment is in order. The State University of New York College at Oswego is an Arts and Sciences College with graduate programs in Art, Chemistry, Education, Human Services/ Counseling, Management, Psychology, School Counselor, and School Psychologist. The College enrolls about 7,500 students, with 360 full-time faculty. The library collection includes 400,000 volumes, 1.5 million microform units, 55,000 audio-visual units and 2,000 active journals. The library staff consists of 18 professionals and 22 support staff employees.

PHILOSOPHICAL RATIONALE FOR DE-EMPHASIS OF DEPARTMENTAL DIVISIONS

Penfield Library began the elimination of traditional divisions between technical services and public services in the early 1970s. During the academic year 1973/1974, the library director implemented the policy which allowed technical services librarians to work at the reference desk. This decision was based primarily upon philosophical, rather than practical, reasons. It was believed that the new policy would help to alleviate the false division between the two departments. The new policy also became an educational experience for all of the librarians. Technical services librarians were able to see more directly the results of their work and improve their cataloging skills.

Reference librarians improved their retrieval skills through an increased understanding of how materials were cataloged and processed. This policy was also based upon the philosophy that librarians should be generalists, possessing knowledge in a variety of areas in addition to that of their specialty. This policy also provided opportunities for the professional development of the staff, whose skills increased, making them more "marketable" and decreasing boredom from repetition of the same old task.

PRACTICAL IMPLICATIONS OF THE NEW POLICY

Although the decision to have technical services staff provide reference service was based upon philosophical reasons, there were some very practical results of the decision. Since the early 1970s, for example, a reference librarian is on the Information Desk all of the hours that the library is open. During the fall and spring semesters the library is open for 95 hours per week, and since there is often more than one reference librarian providing service at one time, 152 hours of reference librarian service are provided. The library began to lose professional staff lines several years after the initial decision to have all librarians provide reference service. Over 20 librarians originally provided reference service, but Penfield was able to maintain this policy, even in the face of staff reduction. From an administrative standpoint, this policy also made it much easier to shift responsibilities among staff members when the need arose due to illness or sabbatical leaves. It has been the library director's experience that individuals who are used to learning and doing new things are less resistant to change and to new ideas.

As technical services staff were becoming involved in reference activities, reference staff were increasing their understanding of technical services operations. Reference librarians had always participated in filing catalog cards in the public catalog, but in the mid to late 1970s, differences between technical services and public services became even less distinct and the involvement of reference librarians in what had traditionally been technical services activities increased significantly.

THE IMPACT OF AUTOMATION
ON LIBRARY SERVICES

The primary cause for this increased involvement has been automation. In 1983 an OCLC terminal was made available at the reference desk. Reference librarians were trained in how to search the online union catalog and in how to interpret MARC records online.

As the library became a participant in the OCLC Serials Control Subsystem and in the Acquisitions Subsystem, reference librarians learned how to search and interpret records specific to those Subsystems as well. In 1985 Penfield Library was a test site for TOMUS, Carlyle Systems' online catalog, which became the library's permanent online catalog after the completion of the test. Now reference librarians were accessing online MARC records that had been edited for local purposes. The most recent technical services automation change for reference librarians was in 1989, when SC350, OCLC's microcomputer based serials control system, became available at the reference desk on a local area network. Reference librarians have complete access to serial holdings statements in the American National Standard (ANSI) format. The addition of OCLC, an online catalog, and SC350 has provided more sophisticated access to library materials. Reference librarians must now understand how library materials are cataloged, classified and indexed and they need the skills to use these automation tools in order to provide the best service to library patrons. This increase in automation has also had an impact on collection development.

The addition of an online catalog with sophisticated indexing has increased the involvement of collection development in cataloging activities. Collection development librarians often request the addition or enhancement of contents notes on the MARC record. Another example of this was provided by a student who was looking for materials on calypso music. A subject search in our online catalog retrieved several hits; when the student set the system to search other libraries which are participants in the online catalog, the student found a record for an additional item. The student submitted an interlibrary loan request, and it was subsequently found that Penfield did own this book but that it was not cataloged with "calypso music" as the subject heading. The book was recataloged and the subject heading was added. Without access to other libraries' holdings the student may never have found this item.

A COMMITMENT TO PROFESSIONAL DEVELOPMENT

The blurring of traditional divisional lines between technical services and reference services departments has enabled changes to be made to many performance programs held by the professional employees. Penfield Library also has prided itself on its commitment towards the professional development of its staff. The library administration has been highly creative and flexible in staff utilization. Individuals who have interests in pursuing various aspects of librarianship outside their job descriptions are provided with opportunities in which to pursue those interests. This emphasis on staff development takes precedence over traditional departmental divisions. In 1983, for example, the library had vacancies for one reference librarian and one technical services librarian. Two candidates who interviewed had interests in both aspects of librarianship. The lines were split so that the two new librarians had responsibilities in reference and technical services. Also, the library currently employs a part time librarian whose time is divided equally between providing reference services and working in the serials department. Another aspect of this staff development centers around individual librarian's subject specialties. As subject specialists the librarians are responsible for collection development. They also serve as department liaisons, teach library instruction classes for departments, and function as reference specialists, regardless of whether the librarians' other responsibilities lie primarily in reference or in technical services. This creative, flexible management style emphasizes commitment to high quality service to patrons and the development of library personnel resources. By pursuing aspects of librarianship in which they have an interest, the staff are better satisfied with their work and more committed to the philosophy of library service.

CROSS-TRAINING ACTIVITIES

While this creative environment is beneficial to both staff and patrons, it does require excellent communication between colleagues and quality training opportunities in order to succeed. Reference and Professional Seminars (RAPS), for example, first began at Penfield in 1973. They were initially intended as opportunities for reference librarians to learn more about specific reference services and sources. Offered several times every semester, RAPS originally centered strictly around the reference department. However, RAPS soon expanded in scope to include other aspects of librarianship such as new services that were available in other library departments or in other departments on campus. In the last three years RAPS have been presented on such technical services topics as the online catalog, AACR2, OCLC, and SC350. RAPS are now presented by any librarian with expertise in a particular area to all other interested staff members.

In addition to RAPS, Penfield Library is involved in other cross-training activities. New librarians who will be providing reference service receive orientation to all areas of the library from those librarians who possess expertise in that area. They are trained by technical services staff in searching OCLC and interpreting MARC records on both OCLC and the online catalog and in using SC350. Another cross-training activity involves a software package entitled CATIE, which allows for local editing of the online catalog. Several staff members whose primary responsibilities lie outside of the technical services department have received training on how to edit our local MARC records using CATIE.

IMPLICATIONS OF THE PENFIELD APPROACH

The advantages to this flexible approach to staff responsibilities are clear. Patrons receive high quality service by having access to a librarian, and library staff have opportunities to pursue a variety of professional interests. While this type of organizational structure has a wide variety of advantages, it does contain several implications for how it is managed. It requires a great deal of cooperation and communication among staff members, and the staff members must themselves be creative and flexible individuals. Because the organizational structure is more like a horizontal line than a hierarchical tree, the librarians who have been successful at Penfield are individuals who, in addition to being flexible, are self-motivated and self-directed, and who do not require a supervisor to set all goals and priorities. In fact, the term "supervisor" is not often used at Penfield to describe the relationships between librarians. Instead, there are four Coordinators who "manage" the operations of Access Services, Reference and Library Instruction, Collection Development and Collection Management.

INSTRUCTION, COLLECTION DEVELOPMENT AND COLLECTION MANAGEMENT

The second major implication is that evaluation of a librarian's performance is more complex. The librarians are evaluated in two ways for both term and continuing appointment and for merit: the library director does his or her own evaluation and so does the five-member Penfield Library Personnel Evaluation Committee. This peer evaluation committee solicits feedback from all of the coordinators of areas in which the individual works. Since so many librarians are active in several areas of library service, this often means that three or four coordinators meet with the Personnel Committee. In addition, the evaluation is based upon how well an individual performs for the level of responsibility held in that area. A cataloger, while expected to meet certain standards for providing reference service, is not expected to be as proficient at the finer points of reference service as a librarian whose primary responsibility is reference. Librarians whose primary areas of responsibility are in reference and instruction are not expected to know the finer points of technical services operations.

The library at SUNY College at Oswego has for several decades maintained a primary emphasis on high quality service. Even though Anne Commerton, the library director who initially began the breakdown of traditional divisional lines between technical services and public services, retired from Penfield Library in fall 1990, the influence that this policy will continue to have on library service is undeniable. We expect that future Penfield staff members will maintain the philosophy that user service is of primary importance, and that the traditional divisions between the two library departments must continue to be blurred so that all librarians can provide the best possible access to library materials.

On Becoming Team Players

Kathleen M. Carney

SUMMARY. Migration from one automated system to another brings with it a very different set of problems than moving from a manual to an online environment. This experience at Boston College was an opportunity for Public and Technical Services staff to become team players working toward the same end goal. Ownership of the database becomes shared, and individual perspectives are broadened. Opportunities are provided to develop new relationships outside the library.

OVERVIEW – BOSTON COLLEGE

During the past three years, there has been a virtual explosion of technology based services at O'Neill Library, Boston College. In addition to expanding more traditional online services such as database searching, the Libraries have migrated to a second generation automated system (Geac to NOTIS), implemented a network of multi-database workstations for patrons, provided enhanced access to materials on order and received and expanded dial-up capability to the online catalog.

In addition to this, the Libraries are currently pursuing agreements to add a multi-database product to interface with the online catalog, provide online access to a table of contents service and load records for all government documents selected by the library.

Each of these undertakings has had a profound and radicalizing effect on the Libraries' service imperative. The rate of change and the expansion and enhancement of the Libraries' technological resources proved compelling inducements to explore alternative means of access and delivery. That gradual blurring of lines be-

Kathleen M. Carney is Head of Cataloging, O'Neill Library, Boston College, Chestnut Hill, MA 02167.

tween technical and public services so often referred to in the litera-ture has given way to a much more compelling partnership among all of the departments involved.

The evolution and cultivation of these partnerships have been both formal and informal. The following presents examples of how the O'Neill Library Cataloging Department and selected public ser-vice departments were able to identify and create opportunities em-phasizing access while utilizing all resources more effectively.

RESOURCES/TECHNOLOGY

NOTIS, of course, was the primary catalyst for change this year. In addition to the internal upheavals of workflow, procedures and training, the NOTIS installation proved to be a very effective cata-lyst for changing how we relate to other departments and other Bos-ton College libraries. The importance of the successful collabora-tion among departments, different libraries and Information Technology during the implementation and installation phase cannot be emphasized enough. These new partnerships have contributed enormously to demystifying the work done in each area. Beyond ensuring the ongoing success and quality of our new online system, these efforts also demonstrated how focusing more on integration rather than differences, fundamentally enhanced all of our service efforts.

Our primary goal is to focus attention on the greater integration of the new system and to use this as a means to explore new ways of sharing tasks across departments to enhance the database and to more effectively exploit the features of our second generation on-line system. Although studies have shown that automating the first time around allows for some staffing reductions in technical ser-vices, any streamlining accomplished during that first generation means staff are spread fairly thin when it comes time to migrate to the second generation system.[1]

ADMINISTRATIVE ISSUES

Posing the question "who owns the database anyway" meant committing the Cataloging Department to a redefinition of our role in providing access and delivery to the Libraries' materials and services. Formally recognizing that the service mission of the Cataloging Department could be more successfully accomplished by broadening our consulting and training responsibilities to Public Service staff was the first step toward integrating our service objectives.

Changing systems has accelerated the evolution and shift from management of the catalog to management of the database by introducing more complex record relationships and more complex online operations such as authority control.[2] These and other database issues were discussed at length in departmental policy meetings and meetings of the Library Automation Coordinating Committee. Catalogers, reference librarians, systems managers and representatives from other Boston College libraries identified a number of projects to collaborate on and set priorities according to a particular project's impact on the access and delivery of service to our users.

Training, scheduling and evaluation were all worked out on a project by project basis. Several general sessions giving an overview of the MARC format and an introduction to other bibliographic standards were presented to public service staff to provide a basis for some of the online catalog work. Technical service staff who were to serve as volunteers in the reference department attended general bibliographic instruction sessions and more specialized training sessions. In each instance, training was viewed as developing skills which should enable the individual to perform tasks to complete a particular project and to participate in similar projects as they are developed.

Cultivating this network of specialists across departments has been one of the most gratifying aspects of integrating our efforts to manage our resources. The benefits realized most quickly have been the immediacy and control of access and delivery, all without compromising the accuracy or integrity of the tools we use.

PARTNERSHIPS AND PROJECTS

Decentralizing some catalog maintenance tasks seemed the most natural place to begin the new partnership process. Even in the previous Geac environment, the Cataloging Department had made arrangements for selected linking tasks to be performed by Reference Department assistants. Building on their knowledge of established holdings conventions we were able to continue this once NOTIS was brought up. Conducting a modified version of the linking training for selected Circulation staff when NOTIS circulation went into production enabled that department to identify and correct item records and then deliver materials to patrons which would formerly have been routed to Cataloging for review.

Additional maintenance tasks were targeted as candidates for reassigning to public service staff at several of the branch libraries. Providing the training and coordination for these other sites to perform such online tasks as changing location codes, creating provisional records for temporary paperback collections, and deactivating holdings statements for missing items, has helped enormously to streamline our branch processing operations and improve the timeliness of information in the online catalog.

An unexpected benefit of these newly developed partnerships proved to be the handling of rush cataloging requests. Since the display of full bibliographic on-order records was a new feature in the Libraries' NOTIS online catalog, requests for this service increased dramatically. During the fall semester, requests had increased approximately 400%. As public service staff became more expert at interpreting holdings and order records, they were better able to channel patron requests to the appropriate department and inform patrons of the status of a particular item. Current receipts, orders pending and bindery information can all be tracked in a much more integrated way, permitting both technical and public service staff to share responsibility for providing the most accurate information to patrons.

While technical service staff struggled to meet the myriad challenges of changing the Libraries' online system, reference staff were also contending with the challenge of doubling Multi-Platter service. Cataloging volunteers have been active participants in assisting the reference staff meet that challenge. During the academic year cataloging staff were regularly scheduled to serve in the electronic reference area and for reference desk duty. This participation has introduced a certain vitality and important dynamic to cataloging policy considerations. This partnership will continue to grow and become even more valuable as we move forward with the implementation of cross references in the online catalog and adoption of the new MARC format for holdings and locations.

FUTURE PLANS

Efforts toward integrating services provided by reference, cataloging and circulation have been very successful thus far. The increased integration of the Libraries' new online system has proved to be a useful model. Building a network of experts has had an impact when considering the implementation of other new services and projects. Scheduled for the coming year are projects to convert and consolidate departmental files for collection development and retention decisions for entry into NOTIS, load records for O'Neill Library's government documents collection into the online catalog and several other database cleanup projects. A current project to create a database of Boston College faculty publications clearly demonstrates the value of past exchanges among cataloging, systems and reference. The retrieval, manipulation and organization of data to be entered into the NOTIS database file will require expertise in several software programs, CD-ROM databases, bibliographic utilities and a variety of technical and bibliographic standards. The fact that these relationships had already been established to address similar issues will certainly contribute to the successful creation of this new database, and more importantly help to reveal other potential applications for this particular technological resource.

CONCLUSION

Examining and redefining roles to provide access and delivery proved indispensable to advancing services this past year. Whether as mundane as consulting on spine labels or as provocative as the Cataloging Department surveying other library departments on their level of satisfaction with Cataloging's services to them, the benefits of seeking new partnerships has been clearly demonstrated. Developing new skills, demystifying the work done in every department, making progress on streamlining selected operations have all contributed to enhancing access and delivery. The Libraries' administrative climate is, of course, critical to the success or failure of these efforts. Fostering a team approach, providing opportunities for convergence, and providing vision which embraces the unconventional have helped to broaden our range of effectiveness. As services and resources continue to expand, libraries must be creative when confronting the added challenge of making effective choices and of providing, more and more, immediate delivery. The differences between reference and technical services have not evaporated, but they can be directed toward maximizing efforts and resources to meet these challenges.

REFERENCES

1. Horny, Karen L. "Fifteen Years of Automation: Evolution of Technical Services Staffing, *Library Resources & Technical Services 31 (January-March 1987)*:69-76.

2. Hill, Janet Swan. "Staffing Technical Services in 1995," *Journal of Library Administration* 9 (1988):97.

Cataloging for Access

Carol Mandel

SUMMARY. There is a new movement afoot to change cataloging philosophy. The aim of library cataloging has been to create a ma-chine-readable card catalog rather than to provide optimum online access for library users. Catalogers need to become operationally engaged in the vision of the "new catalog," and take advantage of the potential of the OPAC. Cataloging for "access" rather than identification should be the motto of Technical Services Divisions in the 1990s. These discussions are already taking place in the Library of Congress, and in such forums as the Technical Services Directors of Large Research Libraries Discussion Group.

OVERVIEW

The online catalog has not slipped through the library door unno-ticed. Much heralded, it has been greeted in individual libraries with highly publicized celebrations and in the library profession with a wealth of literature and research. The potential of the OPAC for extending bibliographical and physical access to materials is well-known and widely discussed; librarians, as represented in their litera-ture and presentations, cannot be faulted for lack of vision. Yet, if one looks beyond the literature, into the back rooms of libraries where the catalog itself is created, is the impact of the online catalog evident? Automation is indeed pervasive. Cataloging workflows, procedures and the nature of copy cataloging are en-tirely different, optimized to take advantage of the freedom from the 3″ × 5″ card. But what of the core function of cataloging, the original creation of the bibliographic record?

Carol Mandel is Director, Technical Services, Columbia University Libraries, New York, NY 10027.

While the intellectual process of original cataloging and its end product have adapted admirably to the production of machine-readable records, they have remained surprisingly unaffected by the environment in which those records are used. The aim of library cataloging continues to be the creation of a machine-readable card catalog rather than to provide optimum online access for library users. This may seem only a semantic distinction, but it is the foundation of a cataloging culture that has not yet become operationally engaged in the vision of the "new catalog." It is a culture not only of catalogers, but of librarians in many specialities whose expectations of the cataloging record have not fully adapted to a new environment.

TRENDS AND ISSUES

What are the relevant trends and issues in this new environment? Here is a partial list:

1. Shared Cataloging

Since the inception of OCLC, shared cataloging has become central to effective library operations. Original cataloging is extremely expensive; this costly resource must be shared. While this is not a post-OPAC phenomenon, the fact that a library is cataloging not only for itself but for others contributes to the expectations of original cataloging.

2. The Nature of Online Catalog Use

The online catalog has made it possible to learn about actual user behavior and needs. Exposed through transaction log studies, users' difficulties with library practices, their errors in spelling and citations and their typically non-methodical approaches to searching fly in the face of librarians' conceptions of the catalog as an orderly, carefully constructed and easy-to-use tool. Users have demonstrated that they need considerable help in searching, especially help in the form of good system design, sample keywords and cross-references — devices that link users' entry vocabulary to catalog records. Good records alone do not meet this need.

3. Subject Searching

The new paradigm revealed by online catalog use studies has been the prevalence of subject searching.[1] This has put library subject cataloging under new scrutiny. Users' abilities (or inclinations) to employ pre-coordinated LC subject headings are limited, and their conceptualizations of subjects are consistently unpredictable. Users' search terms are rarely exact matches to subject headings in the catalog.

4. The "Whole Earth" Catalog

The individual online library catalog is a subset of a virtual national and, increasingly, international database. At some library sites it is already possible for users to search multiple catalogs, and seamless interfaces to move users among catalogs are in the design phase. The catalog no longer functions only "to show what the library has . . . " (Cutter's second objective), but to show what the library can obtain for the user. The catalog records created by a library must fit into this larger universe.

5. The Supercatalog

Many online catalogs have already been expanded to include abstract and index records obtained from a variety of sources. Library catalogs will no longer consist solely of records created and controlled by the library. In this context, differences in principle and practice between library cataloging and commercial indexing will be, at best, meaningless to users; at worst, these differences will be an impediment to access. To add to the complexity, libraries have also begun to make full text and other non-bibliographic files accessible directly through the online catalog.

6. The Format Explosion

Print on paper is still the most prevalent form of recorded knowledge, but new electronic and magnetic formats abound and must be cataloged if they are to be accessible. At the same time, new methods of research and emerging disciplines rely increasingly on non-book collections, with concomitant demands to include these collections in the library catalogs. The pressure is on to catalog more, and to do so with a wider range of expertise as each format presents unique problems.

7. The Version Explosion

The introduction of new media, changes in publishing patterns, reproduction for preservation, and electronic document preparation are some of the factors leading to an ever-widening variety of formats/editions/versions in which a particular work may appear. And the "whole earth catalog" is much more likely to include many versions of a particular work than is the single library catalog in isolation. The profession has recently developed a strategy for addressing some aspects of this problem, but much work remains to be done before multiple versions in the broadest sense are easily accessed in large databases. At the same time, the traditional role of descriptive cataloging to specify a particular edition must be considered in a new context.

8. Online Inventory Control

In most libraries, the online public catalog does not stand alone but is a module of an integrated system. The parent system supports a variety of library processes and record-keeping functions, all associated with a single bibliographic database. In these systems, the catalog record is closely linked to detailed information about individual pieces (typically identified by barcode numbers on the items). Overseeing the creation and maintenance of this piece-level information is a responsibility that often falls to catalogers. Thus, the cataloger is faced with demands on the micro-level as well as the macro-level of the catalog's new scope.

IMPACT ON TECHNICAL SERVICES

The impact of these trends has been recognized by theorists. In fact, it has inspired some to propose a re-conceptualization of library cataloging. Wilson has recommended an entirely changed approach to descriptive cataloging based on cataloging the work rather than the piece at hand.[2] The call to abandon LCSH in favor of a modern thesaurus is often heard.[3] But it is not surprising that little action has been taken along these drastic lines. The investment in existing records, existing databases and existing standards is enormous. The move to the future must protect this investment. The most promising proposal yet to appear has been put forward by Duke[4] who envisions a three-part structure for the catalog record: (a) a document surrogate, much like today's catalog record but potentially leaner, (b) a document guide that provides the structure to enter enriched data, such as tables of contents, summary notes, back-of-book indexes, etc., and (c) the document text itself. This proposal begins to grapple in a realistic way with an approach to the enriched, expanded, multi-tiered catalog.

The fact that Duke's proposed first tier is much like today's catalog record need not be construed to imply that library cataloging does not need to change. The resources available for library cataloging are not likely to expand and yet the demands posed by the trends just described are both enormous and compelling. If librarians are to eke out the support and professional energy to meet these demands, it will be necessary to make the work of creating the "document surrogate" as streamlined and cost effective as possible. And the profession must divert some, ideally much, of the talent and energy that now labors over these records to meeting new demands instead. This will require a change in the cataloging culture, a shift in emphasis from creating library catalogs to cataloging for access.

There has long been in the library profession an interest in making the cataloging process as efficient as possible.[5] Yet at the same time, creating machine-readable records for a shared cataloging environment has added complexity to original cataloging. Name authority work now requires fitting headings into a national database, rather than a smaller local one. National standards must be followed if the same records are to be used by many libraries. And the MARC record has more fields than a $3'' \times 5''$ card. Unfortunately, the profession has encouraged cataloging to be overtaken by such complexity even when it is not necessary. In the drive to assure that records are consistent in a national database, a crucial question has been overlooked: What difference does this consistency make?

Gregor and Mandel have argued that there are many parts of the catalog record where consistency between catalogers does not matter, and that professional and intellectual energy is spent unnecessarily on contriving and following rules to achieve a level of consistency not required for access or identification of titles.[6] In descriptive cataloging, this is manifested in the proliferation of Rule Interpretations; in subject analysis it takes the form of a time-consuming and unproductive quest for the "right" subject heading.

Tucker has observed that when Library of Congress Rule "Interpretations are created changed, or abolished, the reason can always be found in the rich source of questions arising in practice under forces of standardization."[7] For the most part, these are questions that have been raised because catalogers are concerned that their decisions about an aspect of a record must be the same as those of catalogers at the Library of Congress. And LC catalogers themselves ask questions for the same reason, concerned that records will match those of their revisors. Yet the cataloging code itself, AACR2, leaves many areas to a cataloger's professional judgement. In creating many parts of the bibliographic record there is no one, right answer, and there are often at least several good answers. It does not matter that cataloger X might transcribe, for example, the publisher's name one way and cataloger Y record it in another; achieving a consistent result does not merit the time taken to seek and digest the relevant Rule Interpretation. Consistency in transcribing a publisher's name does not affect access. Viewed in today's environment of modern publishing, multiple versions and wide variations among libraries in their guidelines for accepting copy cataloging, such consistency also does little, if anything, to aid in the identification of an edition. While consistency in authority work (i.e., identifying the correct author in the authority file) is critical to access in the online catalog, many aspects of descriptive cataloging do not require all catalogers' work to be predictably the same. The profession has created a culture in which catalogers feel they must spend an inordinate amount of time asking questions and looking up answers in an effort to achieve a dubious objective.

A similar problem hampers subject cataloging. It is an unrealistic goal to attempt to collocate consistently all books on a particular topic under a single subject term. Each book is unique in its approach to and interpretation of a "particular" subject. Subject analysis is necessarily subjective. Indexers have long understood that only a reasonable degree of interindexer consistency can ever be achieved. More important, the likelihood that a reader will use the same term for a topic as that applied by the cataloger is small. Bates cites studies that, taken together, indicate that the likelihood that any two people will use the same term for a concept or a book is 10%-20%.[8] Subject searching by its nature is inexact and exploratory. A comprehensive subject search requires multiple routes. It is much more important to subject access to provide a well designed online system, cross-references that aid in selecting terms, and a few thoughtfully selected subject headings than it is to seek the "right" heading for an item. Catalogers are expected to spend time constructing arcane LC subject strings, time that would be better directed toward, for example, improving LCSH cross reference displays in the online catalog.

In both descriptive cataloging and subject analysis, this unnecessary quest for precision and consistency has created a cataloging culture that expends professional judgement on rule-making rather than on badly needed problem solving. On the operational level, catalogers are pushed to expend more time than is productive in creating individual records – time better spent on providing access to a greater number of items or on extending the coverage of the catalog in new ways. On broader professional and planning levels, the country's most knowledgeable catalogers spend many hours in meetings (and many days in related preparation) crafting and debating rules and rule interpretations that make no significant difference to bibliographic access. This expertise and energy should instead be focused on meeting the many challenges posed by the "new catalog."

CONCLUSIONS

Redirecting the existing cataloging culture will require a paradigm shift throughout the profession – not just among the catalogers. Reference librarians often have unrealistic expectations of the catalog, particularly in the area of subject collocation.[9] But the greatest pressure is placed on catalogers by each other. Each trainer/revisor expects the junior cataloger's records to be formulated exactly as the trainer would predict; each senior cataloger strives to create a record that would be exactly as an LC cataloger would provide; each LC cataloger strives to match the exact judgement of his/her revisor. The entire profession will need to agree on those (many) areas of the record where consistency does not matter and accept the judgement of the individual professional cataloger who creates the initial record. This sounds deceptively simple, but requires a fundamental change in the way both reference librarians and catalogers view the catalog. The online catalog environment places new demands on catalogers' judgement and creativity. The profession should free catalogers to meet those demands.

REFERENCES

1. Pauline Cochrane, "A Paradigm Shift in Library Science," *Information Technology and Libraries* (2) 1: 3-4, 1983.

2. Patrick Wilson, "The Second Objective," in *The Conceptual Foundations of Descriptive Cataloging*, edited by Elaine Svenonius (San Diego, CA: Academic Press, 1989), pp. 5-16.

3. For reviews of criticism of LCSH see Robert Holly and Robert Kielheffer, "Is There an Answer to the Subject Access Crisis?" *Cataloging & Classification Quarterly*(1)2/3: 125-133, 1982 and Pauline Cochrane and Monika Kirkland, *Critical Views of LCSH: A Bibliographic Essay* (Syracuse, N.Y., 1981). Available from ERIC Clearinghouse on Information Resources, ED 208 900.

4. John Duke, "Access and Automation: The Catalog Record in the Age of Automation," in *The Conceptual Foundations of Descriptive Cataloging*, edited by Elaine Svenonius (San Diego, CA: Academic Press, 1989), pp. 117-128.

5. A good example of such an effort at the Library of Congress is described in Martha Yee, "Attempts to Deal with the 'Crisis in Cataloging' at the Library of Congress in the 1940s," *Library Quarterly* (57) 1:1-31, 1987.

6. Dorothy Gregor and Carol Mandel. Presentation at meeting of Technical Services Directors of Large Research Libraries Discussion Group, American Library Association Midwinter Meeting, January 1990. Expanded version for publication is in process. The two paragraphs which follow are excerpted from the paper in process.

7. Ben R. Tucker, "Ask Me No Questions and I'll Write You No RIs," in *The Conceptual Foundations of Descriptive Cataloging*, edited by Elaine Svenonius (San Diego, CA: Academic Press, 1989), pp. 45-50.

8. Marcia Bates, "Designing online catalog subject access to meet user needs," in *55th IFLA Council and General Conference, Paris, France, 8/19-26. Division of Bibliographic Control. Section on Classification and Indexing* (The Hague, Netherlands: IFLA, 1989), pp. 40:24-40:26.

9. An example of this viewpoint can be found in Constance McCarthy, "A Reference Librarian's View of the Online Subject Catalog," *Cataloging & Classification Quarterly* (10) 1/2:203-211, 1989.

Automation, Barriers, and Communication: How an Integrated Library System Changes Public Services-Technical Services Relationships

Alice J. Allen

SUMMARY. Implementation of an integrated library system can cause re-examination of long-standing barriers between technical services and public services. The stakes are high and both sides experience stress while learning the new system and interpreting it to patrons. The University of Oregon Library, through both failures and successes, is learning how to use automation to change and improve technical services-public services communication. The article concludes with suggestions on what both sides can do to break down traditional barriers.

Introducing automation, specifically an integrated library system, into a traditionally organized library, can have interesting consequences. In addition to the technological travails of acquiring a system and making it work, librarians are also questioning traditional public services/technical services differences and whether those differences continue to serve the profession effectively. The existence of what we have all assumed were permanent barriers between the

Alice J. Allen is Assistant University Librarian for Technical Services, University of Oregon Library, Eugene, OR 97403.

Revision of a presentation to the ALCTS Technical Services Administrators of Medium-sized Research Libraries Discussion Group, June 23, 1990.

two aspects of library service is now being challenged. The experience of the University of Oregon Library in this respect, though not unique, can serve as an example of the stresses and rewards that can result from such self-examination.

Most of us can describe differences between technical services and public services world views, both from reading the literature and from our own experience as well. But *differences* aren't necessarily the same as *barriers*. I don't find it a bad thing that there are differences, or distinctions. But distinctions become barriers when they inflate to the point of obscuring what we have in common.

Maybe we should have been worrying more about barriers in the past, but automation has forced us to take a fresh look at everything. Once a library has automated, the public services-technical services dynamic is bound to change. Unfortunately, change can go either way and barriers can be created or reinforced, as well as broken down.

Anyone who has worked in a library during the time an integrated library system is being brought on line knows the cost of such a project, in dollars and in staff time. Typically these efforts may take a year or more to complete. Not only are systems expensive, patron interest in them is extremely high; they love them intensely but they also scrutinize them exhaustively and ask many questions.

Thus the automation process makes everyone acutely aware that the stakes are very high. Technical services staff must keep the system up and running at 100% reliability, and insure that the data base is perfect in every way. Public services people have to explain (sometimes defend) a system they may not fully understand and which seems to change rapidly, even capriciously. No wonder the question of barriers becomes so important. From a purely pragmatic point of view, if nothing else, we *need* each other to make this enterprise, on which we have staked so much, a success.

FIRST STEPS AND FAILURES

These questions are still painfully new at the University of Oregon; we brought the final piece of our first integrated library system on line in March 1990. However, you could say that at the University of Oregon we've been sneaking up on automation for quite a while. The Library installed Innovacq in 1983, the Innovacq serials control module in 1986, the Innopac online catalog in December 1988 and circulation in March 1990. We're still on a learning curve and will be for some time. We've had successes and failures, which is to say, we're normal.

One of our conspicuous failures occurred when we implemented Innovacq serials control. A decision was made to give highest priority during the implementation phase to maintaining rapid turnaround time on checking in current issues. This was done, but it meant creating online records in extreme haste, and without careful consideration of data input standards. The result was a data base of about 18,000 records that featured missing, incomplete, or inaccurate holdings data, inaccurate binding and claiming parameters, and insufficient access points to allow efficient record retrieval and check in. Relationships between public services and technical services became strained as public services staff became aware that they could not rely on Innovacq to tell them what they and their patrons needed to know. An early attempt at an Innovacq users group with technical and public services participants sputtered and ultimately failed, leaving everyone more disgruntled than before.

WHOLE-LIBRARY PARTICIPATION

We were determined to do things better with Innopac (or Janus, our local name for the system), and not repeat our mistakes. From the beginning, we took several steps to encourage whole-library participation.

A Steering Committee with public services and technical services representatives, charged with overseeing the implementation process, was established as soon as the contract with the vendor was signed. This committee met once or twice a week for about 2 1/2 years. Nine subcommittees, staffed with volunteers from the Library staff, were also appointed. Everyone who volunteered received an assignment. Each subcommittee, including those dealing with technical topics like mapping of MARC fields into appropriate system indexes, had both public and technical services members.

A series of meetings for all staff were held to provide input on important decisions like indexing the data base, display formats, and changes in circulation policy and procedure.

Technical Services staff began issuing three publications for the Library staff. The first was *Cardbusters*, designed to inform staff of the progress of the implementation project and answer questions about the system. The second was *Access*, published at irregular intervals by the Systems Office to discuss system problems and questions and pass along statistics on system use and performance. *Access* also discusses microcomputing topics of general interest. The third publication was *Question: Authority*, a monthly publication of the Authority Section of the Catalog Dept. to alert staff to database problems, announce major updates and fixes that have been completed, mention interesting new subject headings, etc.

All three publications have been enthusiastically received by Library staff. *Cardbusters*, never intended to be a permanent publication, ceased after the system was fully implemented. The other two are ongoing.

After the implementation phase, a Database Coordination Group was established to discuss and make recommendations on a variety of issues related to creation and maintenance of the data base. The Group includes reference librarians, technical services staff, and the coordinators of library instruction and of online searching. Meeting times and agendas are published in advance and all interested staff are encouraged to attend.

Each department in the Library now has its "Janus liaisons" — staff who are trained by the Systems Office to do first-line troubleshooting for terminal and system problems. This helps an overworked systems staff and insures that every department has two people (liaison and backup) who know more about the system than the average staff member. The liaison scheme helps staff to know what information is needed by the Systems Office when problems occur.

I think all these things have been very successful in developing a feeling of ownership of the system throughout the Library. I did not anticipate, nor did I in fact detect, any resentment or protectiveness on the part of technical services staff. In fact, many technical services staff feel that increased information sharing has provided a base of library-wide support for allocation of resources to data base quality.

DEALING WITH CONFLICTS

In spite of our precautions there have been problems. One of the most sensitive incidents could be called the Current Periodicals List controversy. For some years the Library has produced a paper list giving brief information on all currently received periodical titles, with call number and the beginning volume of the subscription. It was a popular tool because it was a quick look-up and allowed users to avoid venturing into the bibliographic maze of the card catalog.

In early 1989, after much discussion, the decision was made to cease producing new editions of the list. Janus offered much more data including up-to-the-minute check-in data. The old lists did remain out for the public, until recently; then, because they had become extremely out of date, they were removed. The uproar was immediate. Patrons and reference librarians wanted their familiar lists back, no matter their flaws.

Public services people thought this was a decision forced by technical services people who knew nothing of the realities of patron service. Technical services staff felt that the public services objections were based on inability or unwillingness to learn how to use the online catalog and interpret its records to patrons.

In spite of the tensions created, both technical services and public services staff worked on ways to deal with patron and staff frustration. Additional staff training sessions were planned, focussing on how to read and interpret serial records in Janus. Improved handouts were designed, including a brief description of searching for periodicals in Janus. Several Janus terminals were relocated from low-use areas to a table near the periodical indexes. Patron complaints have subsided. However, this episode seems to be a microcosm of issues that influence barriers between technical and public services. We realized that although we were doing better, we had more to learn.

At this point in our library's experience with automation, I feel able to risk some generalizations about the breaking down of barriers. Each "side" can do specific things to keep the process moving and make it successful.

WHAT TECHNICAL SERVICES STAFF CAN DO

Technical services staff can start by making an effort to understand how public services staff set priorities. It is a very different process from that employed in technical services, heavily influenced by the pragmatic requirements of life on the front lines. I can see that in some respects our priorities will move closer together over time, but will never entirely converge.

In that context, technical services staff should consider, when appropriate, strategic abandonment of some dearly held principles of bibliographic control — know when to hang on and when to yield gracefully if patrons might benefit. Public services staff will learn, through using the system, the importance of care and accuracy in the many small things that contribute to data base maintenance. In return, technical services staff should learn to be flexible when possible.

It is important that technical services staff be willing and prepared to share information with their public services colleagues. Sharing of information should be done professionally, without condescension, and without making the content seem more complicated than it really is. Communications should be repeated as often as necessary to insure understanding. None of us learned to understand the MARC format, successive vs. latest title serial cataloging, or the relationship between bibliographic data and holdings data in an OPAC, in 15 minutes.

WHAT PUBLIC SERVICES STAFF CAN DO

Public services staff can also make special contributions to the process of breaking down barriers. The most important of these is to share information with technical services colleagues on how patrons use and react to the library's online catalog. To be most useful, information on patron use of OPACs should be provided comprehensively, not selectively. The more straightforward and candid public services staff are about their experiences, the more useful their observations will be.

Technical services people have a right to know how the system is being described to patrons, both in formal and informal settings; we have a right to know how well public services people understand the system and how well they convey this to patrons. Important decisions about the data base may depend on how well we understand the system itself, our patrons, and each other.

As obvious as this observation may appear, public services staff must be willing to learn if technical services staff are willing to teach. Indifference, whether articulated or concealed, encourages the continued existence of barriers. Pleading the press of other duties as a reason for not learning more about the system is another way of saying that the educational process is not a high priority.

Finally, public services staff should make sure that technical services staff can count on their support for high standards in the creation and maintenance of the data base. This is not always easy; questions of resource allocation and prioritizing work can be involved. Knowledgeable and appreciative public services colleagues are a tremendous asset to the work of technical services staff members.

It is the responsibility of both technical services and public services librarians to be willing to enter into dialogue, both to talk and to listen. Everyone needs to understand that providing information to one's counterparts is time-consuming if done well. It cannot be "squeezed in" as an afterthought. It should be planned for and assigned an appropriate priority.

STRATEGIES FOR ELIMINATING BARRIERS

What are some strategies for achieving the disappearance of barriers? I don't have all the answers, but here are a few suggestions.

First I should say, as a self-confessed conservative, that I am not enthusiastic about redefining jobs, or job sharing and trading responsibilities to experience first-hand how the other half lives — although those decisions will always be dependent on the needs of the specific organization, not general theory. So far, in the situations most familiar to me, I can still see value in developing and encouraging specialists, meaning *specialists in their jobs* who nevertheless have an organic view of the library itself and its mission. We are all information experts; communication is our stock in trade. We need to practice our communication skills on each other and simply determine that we *will* sustain a mutually rewarding relationship with our counterparts in other divisions.

An understanding of how the library patron interacts with the automated system is the shared, essential factor in eliminating barriers. There has been much written in the literature about unwillingness of technical services librarians to share their expertise about bibliographic control and automation, exhorting public services librarians to stand up for their rights to be involved. The reverse is true as well: public services librarians sometimes reserve for themselves the mystique of being the only ones who know how patrons behave. Instruction is one of the keys to resolving the communications gap. I strongly believe that technical services staff should be heavily involved in the planning and carrying out of library instruction and the preparation of instructional materials of all kinds. This goes not only for instruction of patrons, but of each other. Cooperative training projects for library staff, planned and carried out by technical and public services librarians together, will do much to break down barriers.

In Tom Peters' book *Thriving on Chaos*, he talks about training. Two of his points seem especially relevant here. "Training is used to herald a commitment to a new strategic thrust,"[1] i.e., when you want to make major changes in the way your organization behaves, training is an essential activity. And "Training is used to teach the organization's vision and values."[2] It's how we impart those values to each other and, therefore, how we break down barriers to understanding.

I believe that we should be reading each other's professional literature more than we do, attending each other's programs at conferences, broadening our perspectives. Then we should use this exposure to other points of view to start informal discussions with colleagues. This interaction could be expanded into shared research and publication projects as well. Over time this addresses the hidden barriers and reservations that linger and exert influence, long after formal organizational barriers are struck down.

I have been making these comments from the perspective of a head of technical services. I believe that technical services and public services heads are in key positions. As members of our respective library administrations, we should be able to understand both the political advantages of disappearing barriers, and the philosophical ones. I can see change happening in my library, and I know it's happening elsewhere too.

REFERENCES

1. Peters, Tom. *Thriving on Chaos: Handbook for a Management Revolution*, (New York: Harper & Row, 1988), p. 393.
2. Ibid., p. 394.

III. THE NEW ACCESS SERVICES

The Climate of Change:
Library Organizational Structures,
1985-1990

Patricia M. Larsen

SUMMARY. Changes in information technology, in institutional or societal imperatives, and in user expectations are forcing library administrators to re-examine not only the library's basic services but also the organizational structures which have been created over time to support those services. Organizational change — particularly structural change — is prescribed. The traditional separation of the two major divisions of libraries, technical services and public services, has often been the focus for discussions of library organizational change. Are libraries modifying their organizational structures? Are models evolving which may be adapted by other libraries? The author reports the results of a recent survey of organizational change in university libraries and describes the changes which are taking place. While the long-standing structures are still largely in place, new alignments of functions and non-traditional work unit groupings are becoming more commonplace.

Patricia M. Larsen is Assistant Director for Access Services, Donald O. Rod Library, University of Northern Iowa, Cedar Falls, IA, 50613.

No matter how a given research library defines its future, collaboration, flexibility, and fluidity will be the key attributes that characterize its operations and services. (Woodsworth et al., 1989, p. 138)

Current library administrations should move quickly to flatten hierarchical structures. (Heim, 1989, p. 199)

Typically identified as the most desirable future is a scenario that includes flexible organizations facilitating staff growth and increased contribution to the university missions. (Webster, 1989, p. 201)

Concerned librarians, charged with charting future directions and strategies, are acutely conscious that today the greatest challenge facing their libraries is change. Changes in information technology, in institutional or societal imperatives, and in user expectations are forcing library administrators to re-examine not only the library's basic services but also the organizational structures which have been created over time to support those services. In the profession's literature, collaboration, flexibility, fluidity, and "flattening the hierarchy" are used repeatedly to describe the characteristics of future library organizations.

Organizational change—particularly structural change—is prescribed. That message is often stated so strongly, one can only imagine that not to do so will place librarians in the dilemma depicted in a Gary Larson Far Side cartoon. The dinosaur convention speaker is addressing a dinosaur audience: "The picture is pretty bleak gentlemen. . . . The world's climates are changing, the mammals are taking over, and we all have a brain about the size of a walnut." While few librarians would admit to having a brain the size of a walnut, either literally or figuratively, they certainly know that the environments in which their libraries operate and the tools with which they work are changing. Libraries and librarians must adapt in order to continue to meet the ever-changing needs of their various constituencies. Librarians' intellectual and creative powers—their leadership abilities—are being taxed perhaps as never before as they attempt to meet the pressing needs of today while simultaneously striving to prepare for an only partially imagined future.

TRADITIONAL DIVISIONS: A FOCUS FOR CHANGE

The traditional separation of the two major divisions of libraries, technical services and public services, has often been the focus for discussions of library organizational change. These divisions evolved because they provided a rational, efficient way to accomplish the very different functions and services characteristically performed in and by libraries. The technical division, charged with acquiring and transforming raw materials into goods, supplies the basic foundation for the services provided by the public arm of the library.

As automated systems have become more pervasive in technical services divisions, intra-divisional change within technical services has been expected to occur. For the most part, changes have related to staffing levels, job descriptions and workflow. More recently as libraries have implemented integrated systems, there has been a growing recognition that the reasons for the historical compartmentalization of work units both within divisions and across divisional lines are fading. This perspective presents both a challenge and an opportunity for library planners. One future paradigm of service illustrates how the present dichotomy of services will become increasingly incongruous and why new structures are needed.

> To move from the older paradigm and its collection building orientation to the newer paradigm with its user-centered focus will plainly require an entirely new approach to organizing the library for its work. The older paradigm, being wedded essentially to a materials' handling rationale, has traditionally been structured and administered as a hierarchical control mechanism over materials-handling processes. In contrast, the newer paradigm emphasizes human needs assessments and personal interaction with users. This will require entirely new arrangements for professional work assignments, reporting, and evaluation, where emphasis will be placed primarily on distributed control and independent judgment and decision-making related to ever-changing needs. (Miksa, 1989, pp. 789-790)

Whether or not one agrees with all aspects of this particular vision, it is clear to many librarians that any future paradigm must be more sharply "user-centered." It is at this point that the traditional divisional structure is at its weakest, for while the divisions have facilitated a logical distribution and grouping of responsibilities and skills, they have also been described as creating "barriers" or "walls," and isolating the technical staff from the end user for whom they produce their goods.

Technology has been predicted as the medium which would "blur the lines," facilitate the movement of staff positions from technical services to public services, or, alternatively, provide for the integration of functions (particularly selection and original cataloging) into other public services departments or divisions. While technology obviously can facilitate such changes, it clearly is not sufficient in and of itself to achieve such results. Librarians, particularly administrators, must assume the responsibility to either modify the existing organizational structures or to create new ones which will adequately support each library's service goals.

How to go about exercising this responsibility is far from clear. The questions far outnumber the available answers: Have the old structures really outlived their usefulness? Can they be modified in such a way that they are capable of increasing organizational flexibility? If radical restructuring is to take place, what will the new organizational forms look like? How does one go about accomplishing either incremental or broad-scale change? What are other libraries doing in respect to modifying their organizational structures? Are models evolving which may be adapted by other libraries? Searching for answers to the last two questions may aid in identifying and validating some of the possible responses that can be made to the more abstract questions.

WHAT IS HAPPENING TODAY?

The fact is that while librarians have long expected that organizational change would accompany the introduction of computer technologies into their libraries, they have been exceptionally slow to make such changes. There are few reports of major organizational changes appearing in the profession's literature. The frequently cited University of Illinois at Urbana-Champaign and Penn State experiences are exceptions. A 1985 Office of Management Studies survey reported that among the 82 responding libraries there had been little change in organizational structures accompanying automation, despite the fact that technology was possibly "rendering their structures ineffective" (Busch, 1985). A more informal survey of 53 college and university library administrators recently concluded essentially the same thing; there was still little evidence to indicate that significant organizational changes were taking place in academic libraries (de Klerk and Euster, 1989).

In another effort to assess the extent to which libraries may have been restructuring since 1985, the author conducted a survey of university libraries in May, 1990. The survey focused on the existence (or non-existence) of public service and technical service divisions within the libraries, and on whether those divisions had undergone changes within the past five years.

The survey asked questions focusing on the existence of basic library functions (such as cataloging, reference, circulation) and attempted to identify their location within the organizational structure. Various aspects of change were investigated, including shifts of functions from one division to the other, the addition of new functions, and changes in divisional titles. The reasons for past changes and the libraries' plans for future changes were requested.

A SNAPSHOT OF THE PRESENT: DIVISIONAL AND FUNCTIONAL ALIGNMENTS

The survey was mailed to 216 academic library administrators. One hundred-eighteen responses were received (representing a 55% response rate). The time period investigated was 1985-1990.

The responding libraries indicated overwhelmingly that technical services and public services divisions will not be added to anyone's endangered species list very soon. Ninety-three libraries (79%) continue to have public services divisions and 95 (81%) libraries have technical services divisions. The divisions may be known by titles differing from the traditional ones, but they are nevertheless essentially technical services and public services divisions. Nine libraries reported having created technical services divisions during the past five years, and six other libraries reported having eliminated such divisions. Eleven libraries reported forming new public services divisions, while four other libraries eliminated divisions. The long-standing divisional structure is still very much an accepted, viable organizational pattern.

Functions included in both the technical and public services divisions are, by and large, the traditional ones. (See Table 1.) Less traditional alignments are represented by a number of technical services divisions which have responsibility for circulation (17 libraries) and interlibrary loan (10 libraries).

Library organizational structures vary considerably in respect to the location of the preservation, systems management and collection management functions. Preservation, while primarily attached to technical services, is also frequently the responsibility of a separate department or staff person, and occasionally is included in collection management. Systems management appears in many instances to be a function either looking for a home, or one which will continue to reside in various locations within libraries, depending upon the size of the library and the extent to which the library has implemented online systems.

Collection development and selection activities are more often associated with public services than with technical services, but it is also an area most often shared between the two divisions, as well as with other departments or divisions. There were also 27 occurrences of separate collection management divisions. Acquisitions, serials ordering and receiving, or preservation were often grouped with the collection function.

Integration of functions was apparent at several points in the survey responses. The number and variety of functions which are shared either between technical and public services or with other organizational units is a measure of this characteristic. (See Table 1.) Additionally, libraries were asked to respond to whether or not they engaged in various practices considered to facilitate across-departmental or divisional line communications. One hundred libraries reported using cross-departmental task forces, 99 reported using cross-departmental standing committees, 43 utilize subject-based assignments across departmental lines, 40 report the existence of split assignments between departments, and 10 practice job rotation between departments.

When asked whether they felt that their libraries had become more integrated since automation, 67% of the respondents from libraries which have online catalogs answered yes; 33% of the respondents felt that their libraries had become neither more nor less integrated.

A SNAPSHOT OF THE RECENT PAST:
NEW OR REALIGNED FUNCTIONS

As might be expected, the functions most often reported as new to the libraries were systems management (31 libraries), database management (17 libraries), and preservation (10 libraries). The total number of new systems installed since 1984 (236 including acquisitions, circulation, serials control, and online catalog modules) indicates the rapidly expanding need that libraries have for managing systems and databases. (See Table 2.)

Many libraries are experimenting with the grouping of major responsibilities. Eighteen reported having moved four or more functions from one division to another; 28 reported having moved at least three; 43 moved at least two functions and 58 libraries reported having moved at least one. Functions most often reassigned from one division to another were collection development (15), circulation (15), acquisitions (14), preservation (13), serials ordering/receiving (11), and systems management (11). Functions moved least often were serials cataloging and online searching.

Cumulatively, technical services divisions had 56 functions moved out, but 31 functions were moved into the divisions. Public services divisions had a total of 43 functions moved to other divisions and received 29 new functions. Net losses for technical services divisions were largely due to the out-migration of acquisitions, serials ordering/receiving, physical processing, systems management, and cataloging. For public services, the net loss was scattered across six functional areas, with only the removal of government documents representing any sizeable reduction attributable to a single function.

Circulation was moved into and out of both technical services and public services divisions. Apparently, libraries are having a difficult time deciding whether to emphasize circulation's public aspects or to align it with its operational kin, the systems and bibliographic control components of technical services.

The increased emphasis on collection management, either through

TABLE 1. Responsibility for Selected Functions Within Library Structures

Function	Technical Services	Public Services	Collection Management	Systems	Other Div./Dept.	Shared: TS/PS Div.	Shared: Other Div.
Acquisitions	85	1	10		6	1	
Serials Order/Rec.	81	3	8		6	5	
Cataloging	92	2		1	6	2	1
Serials Cataloging	95	2			6		
Processing	88	1	3	1	7	3	1
Database Maintenance	86	1		3	6	4	3
Systems	37	7		26	27	4	1
Preservation	54	6	3		16	6	5
Gov. Docs.	5	77			11	8	1
Collection	12	25	27		11	14	14
Biblio. Instruction		86	1		10	4	2
Circulation	17	73			11	2	
On-line searching	1	84	1		9	7	1
Reference		87			10	4	2
Interlibrary Loan	10	80			12		

TABLE 2. Status of Automated Systems In Libraries

System	Number Installed	Number Implemented Since 1984	Percent Implemented Since 1984	Libraries Without systems	Number* New Systems Planned
Online Catalog	96	73	76%	22	24
Circulation	97	56	58%	21	33
Acquisitions	74	51	69%	44	43
Serials Control	71	56	79%	47	39

* Includes both first time and later generation systems.

the creation of a new division, or through decentralization, was clearly a moving force during 1985-1990. Collection management divisions received 29 functions which were moved from other divisions. These included not only the selection and collection functions but, in some instances, acquisitions and preservation.

TECHNOLOGY AS A CHANGE AGENT

The majority of the libraries had four or more automated systems. Eighty-one percent of the libraries had online catalogs, 82% had circulation systems, 63% had acquisitions systems, and 60% had serials control systems.

The prevalence of integrated systems is somewhat less, with only 57% of the catalogs including items on order, 59% including items in process, 47% including serials check-in. Eighty-eight percent of the online catalogs also included circulation system information. Only 34% of the online catalogs included all four types of information: on-order, in-process, serials check-in, and circulation status. As more libraries implement integrated systems it can be expected that organizational structures will be affected in a parallel fashion. At present, most libraries are still far from realizing the full powers and impact of a truly integrated system.

FACTORS CONTRIBUTING TO CHANGE

Libraries reported the reasons for change on two different levels. The principal reasons cited for moving individual functions were to provide for a closer relationship with other similar functions, to create a new division, to increase the integration of functions and services, to balance the workload, and to improve the workflow, efficiency, and quality of work performed.

On a broader plane, thirty-seven libraries reported that changes were due to library-wide reorganization. The leading reasons for the reorganizations were cited as: changes in administration (37); to achieve increased efficiency (32); to improve services (32); the introduction of an online system (18); and economic conditions (7).

If libraries have not yet reorganized, many of them are considering the possibility. Twenty-three libraries indicated that they were planning to move staff, functions, or departments between technical services and public services divisions. Another 32 libraries indicated that they had no specific plans at the time but that they expect that such changes will become desirable within the next three years. Many of these libraries were the ones expecting to implement new systems within the same time period.

A ROSE BY ANY OTHER NAME?
OR, WHAT IS IN A NAME?

The names given to the divisions provide another perspective on their character and role within the organizational structures. Technical services divisions are identified by 22 different titles. Eighty percent of the technical services divisions have titles which include the word "technical." There were eight variations of these titles with many compound titles such as "Technical Services and Automation." Other titles indicated that technical services were being redefined to communicate expanded or redefined roles. Examples of these are "Information Access Services" and "Resource Management." The word "access" appears in 11% of the titles and in six different forms. Seven percent of the division titles included the word "collection."

Public services divisions are known by twenty-three different titles. The majority of titles still include the word "public"; 59% of the divisions are included in this group. Other words emphasized in the division titles are information, reference, and collections. Interestingly enough, there were also three public services division titles which included the word "access." Evidently both divisions claim something in the word "access" which describes their respective roles within the library. A few titles focused on the user; "User services," "User Services and Collection Development" and "Reference and User Education" are examples of these.

Name changes were definitely an element in the reorganizations and functional shifts within libraries from 1985-1990. Twenty-one technical services division names were changed, and eleven of the former titles eliminated were ones which included the word "technical." Nineteen public services divisions experienced name changes, with 10 departing from the title of "Public services."

THE OTHER TWENTY PERCENT:
ON THE CUTTING EDGE

What are the characteristics of the atypical libraries—the 19% to 21% that do not have technical services or public services divisions? Obviously, size may explain why some of the libraries do not have divisions, but it is not clear when size is perceived to make divisions organizationally feasible or desirable. For example, two libraries in the 700,000 to 950,000 volume range, with staff sizes ranging from 85 to 120 have changed from divisionalized to departmentalized structures reporting to the director. On the other hand, two libraries of similar size are considering creating divisions.

Four libraries which eliminated only technical services divisions did so by dividing functions between new collection management divisions and either public services or a bibliographic control service division. (Again, the emphasis on collection management programs was a pervasive theme throughout the survey responses.) In one library, cataloging was placed in "Informational and Access Services" (formerly "Public Services") on the "grounds that access begins with the bibliographic record."

Where there was no public services division (but a centralized technical services), the trend was towards divisional or branch library arrangements which were almost entirely public service in nature.

Nine of the larger libraries reported having eliminated their technical services and public services divisions. Reasons, when given, were most often "integration" or "flattening the organization." One librarian wrote "Our aim in organization of the library was to eliminate all distinctions between public services and technical services." In this same library the current periodicals service desk was moved from public services to acquisitions in order to provide a public function to that department, which was described as consistent with the library's holistic philosophy, one which was practiced both organizationally and in job descriptions.

In some libraries the span of control is truly amazing, with twelve to seventeen department heads reporting to the director. How these libraries define "control" and how they deal with the difficulties usually predicted for such a multiplicity of connections to a single

administrator is not known. One library director who had eliminated the divisions in his library is now considering further reorganization because his library is growing and the span of control is
becoming too great.

Other libraries have limited the span of control by combining
technical services and public services into one very large division,
or by recombining them into new, larger, and fewer departments.

Librarians in this group, particularly from the larger libraries,
provided evidence of having given much thought to searching for
new forms of organizational structures designed to meet their library's individual philosophy or mission. Evidence of this thought-
fulness is conveyed by one librarian who reported on the search for
that "effective structure to deliver information" on his campus.
"We want to establish information centers if there is a proven or
perceived need and not be confined by the current branch configura-
tion. The Central site will be like a command center, housing most
of the materials and staff, and connecting to the information centers
via telenetwork. The issue of organizational change has to come
about as a result of the ever-changing way information is stored,
organized, and delivered, and there is not one model that will meet
the needs of patrons for an extended period of time."

CONCLUSIONS

Have the old structures outlived their usefulness? The survey
results indicate that the traditional divisional structure continues to
provide an efficient platform for supporting library services. However, the responsibilities delegated to both technical and public services are being shifted and their respective roles within the library
changed. The driving force for such changes is most often rooted in
the continuing search for efficient organizational models. Despite
the purported user-benefits of holistic librarian models, most libraries are not yet ready to depart from the proven economies of
specialization and grouping of like functions.

Can the old structures be modified in such a way that they are
capable of increasing organizational flexibility? Structures are being
modified for a variety of reasons, but whether the current changes
will increase the organization's capability for flexibility and fluidity

cannot be known at this time. The fact that librarians are modifying structures in a variety of ways should foster an environment more supportive of flexibility.

The built-in limitation of the divisional structure, the "barriers issue," is being moderated in many libraries by the extensive use of committees and task forces which cross departmental or divisional lines. In some instances, split assignments may also be helping to bring technical services staff closer to the user. While such practices may help to communicate and to develop a cohesive library-wide vision, they do not necessarily ensure increased flexibility.

If radical restructuring is to take place, what will the new organizational forms look like? "Radical restructuring" is occurring in relatively few libraries, and each restructuring has been unique to the individual library's mission and situation. If librarians become serious about designing organizational structures to match their service priorities, then it can be expected that the number of models should be limited only by the constraints of imagination and economics. Paradoxically, the new paradigms proposed by Miksa and others have not provided the motivation for many of the recent changes. Quite the contrary is true. The older paradigm with its "collection building orientation" and "materials' handling rationale" (Miksa, 1989, p. 789-790) is much more closely related to the movements for creating collection management, preservation, and systems management divisions or departments. Continued commitment to the older paradigm must explain in part why "radical restructuring" has taken place in so few libraries.

Librarians and libraries clearly are responding to the climate of change that surrounds them. Organizational structures are being re-examined and, in some instances, re-structured. The extent to which re-structuring has taken place is closely related to where libraries are located along the continuum of technological change. One of the most surprising survey results was the discovery that so few libraries have systems installed which provide an integrated approach to the various forms of information. The integration of information is essential in order for the long-predicted "blurring of lines" to take place. While increased integration is perceived to have occurred and changes have been made which promote that concept, the basic technology necessary to support further integration is not yet in place. The difficulties inherent in implementing new systems continue to demand a significant proportion of the organization's resources.

A climate of change surrounds libraries, and as more of the elements move into place, library organizational structures will continue to adapt and assume new forms. Both the variety and quantity of changes being made in libraries affirm that librarians are most assuredly capable of meeting the challenges of the future.

REFERENCES

Busch, B. J. (1985). Automation and Reorganization of Technical and Public Services. Washington, D. C.: Office of Management Studies.

de Klerk, A. and Euster, J. R. (1989). Technology and Organizational Metamorphoses. Library Trends, 37, 457-468.

Heim, K. M. (1989). The New Prime Directive: User Convenience. The Journal of Academic Librarianship 15, 198-199.

Miksa, F. (1989). The Future of Reference II: A Paradigm of Academic Library Organization. College and Research Libraries News, 50, 780-790.

Webster, D. E. (1989). Closing the Gap Between Desirability and Achievability. The Journal of Academic Librarianship, 15, 200-201.

Wordsworth, A., Allen, N., Hoadley, I., Lester, J., Molholt, P., Nitecki, D., & Wetherbee, L. (1989). The Model Research Library: Planning for the Future. The Journal of Academic Librarianship, 15, 132-138.

From Binomial to Trinomial: The Entrance of Collection Development into the Public/Technical Services Equation

Gillian M. McCombs

SUMMARY. The relationship between Public and Technical Services has been a constant topic in the professional literature through the years. However, this relationship is moving to a new dimension. Automation has paved the way for the entrance of a new player— Collection Development. By rethinking categories and transcending boundaries, libraries as a whole will be empowered to serve their clients in a way more suited to the technology and the demands of the year 2000. A change in service orientation and attitude will redefine job descriptions and relationships, as libraries will in the future be defined by the services they give, not the size of their collections or the numbers of staff.

INTRODUCTION

In 1984, Jim Neal, Dean of Libraries at Indiana University and then Assistant Dean of Reference at Penn State, presented a paper at the ASIS Annual Meeting in Philadelphia on the public services/ technical services interaction. His title was "And the walls came tumblin' down".[1] The paper provides an excellent starting point for a fresh look at the perennial public/technical services dialogue.

The relationship between the two traditional divisions of library functions is moving to a new dimension. Instead of the traditional

Gillian M. McCombs is Assistant Director for Technical Services and Systems at the University at Albany, State University of New York, 1400 Washington Ave., Albany, NY 12222.

bifurcate split, public services and technical services librarians are being joined by collection development librarians in a three part harmony. A new working relationship is being shaped where technical services librarians are not just catalogers, public services librarians are more than reference librarians and bibliographers do more than select books.[2]

Life was not always thus. Some of you may have forgotten how things used to be, and some of you may be privileged enough to have started professional life in this new era. Here is a reminder of the "old days," from an issue of *American Libraries*, written just over 10 years ago, by that most eminently quotable librarian Michael Gorman.

> And it came to pass that when Kutta the Book God had made the first Library, she saw that it was good. She called the librarians together and divided them as a herder divides the sheep and the goats. To the first group she spoke, saying 'You shall dwell in the light and serve the readers, and your glory shall be great.' Then she turned to the second group and spoke, saying 'You shall dwell in the darkness. Secret shall be your ways and hidden your practices. You shall not know the public, neither shall any reader know you. Go forth and classify.'[3]

AUTOMATION AS THE CATALYST FOR CHANGE

Practical experience, and numerous articles on the topic demonstrate not that lines are blurring but that very definitely barriers are being broken down, and that the chief catalyst for this happening is automation, both the automation of technical services processing and administrative functions, and the automation of the traditional information seeking and information providing mechanisms used in public services, all of them now coming together in a truly integrated online library information system.

In the early 1980s, the ideal we were working toward was the "ecumenical librarian"[4]—who both cataloged and did reference work, and who used knowledge gained in one role to enhance understanding of the other. This model was adapted with considerable success at larger institutions such as Penn State[5] and the University of Illinois at Urbana-Champaign.[6] Richard De Gennaro has just announced a new organizational structure for Harvard College which is quite similar.[7] There are also many smaller libraries where staff have consistently fulfilled both functions and there are many advantages to this duality.[8] In practice however, this model is neither a realistic nor a practical goal for a medium-sized research library. The concept of departmental subject expertise residing in one person/team/department to both catalog and provide reference service has several key roadblocks to success. First, the level of cataloging expertise needed to do original cataloging is extremely high. It is not a skill that can be taught in a day or even a week. It is a craft that, once learned, needs to be kept up and constantly updated or skills are lost and rule interpretations missed. Second, many catalogers have some subject expertise, can answer some general reference questions, and can certainly assist patrons in using the online catalog, but extensive training is required to enable them to answer many standard patron queries. A direct exchange of staff resources between technical services and reference will always result, in the beginning, in a loss of service and fewer books cataloged. It requires a definite long-term commitment to absorb this in order to reap the future benefits.[9]

WORKFLOW CHANGES

The interests of our patrons are best served by a new relationship which neither polarizes nor politicizes the questions of access, a tripartite relationship with the new player being Collection Development. By becoming organizationally "multilingual,"[10] we can break down all the old barriers, look for opportunities instead of problems, and invent new combinations of functionality.

Automation has given us the capability for developing our potential to "think across boundaries . . . to see problems and opportunities integratively . . . rather than dividing information and experience into discrete bits assigned to distinct, separate categories that never touch one another."[11] The changes in workflow in technical services illustrate this point. Traditional work flow in a semi-automated library shows material being ordered, received and cataloged

(Diagram A). The books and bibliographic records make their separate ways to the patron. In a revised workflow pattern utilizing a fully integrated library information system (Diagram B), a circular model can be used. At the very center is shown the ordering of materials, moving out to materials received, cataloged locally and available nationally. The functions can be performed anywhere within the library where there is a terminal, and even off campus. Library systems have now developed so that an item can be searched first during the collection development process, the record found subsequently used for ordering and invoicing, for receipt and claiming, and then for cataloging—the work being done perhaps by a former acquisitions staff member not necessarily a cataloger. Workflow in many Technical Services departments has changed to reflect this shift.[12] The role of Collection Development has been highlighted, whilst the role of cataloging (at least copy cataloging) has become less important.

Online library information systems provide the framework for these two versions of workflow. In the first scenario cataloging is done on the utility, the bibliographic records are loaded into the cataloging subsystem, it goes through catalog maintenance and into the online catalog (Diagram C). A parallel flow through happens with circulation information. The student database feeds into the patron database, forming part of the circulation subsystem which matches item/charge information with the bibliographic record. Subsystems such as acquisitions, serials control and reserve have frequently been stand alone systems, not connected to the online catalog, and often only accessed by a separate terminal or by going out of the online catalog and into a separate sub-system.

In the second scenario, the new version of an online system resembles more a Wheel of Fortune than a series of connected boxes (Diagram D). The first use of the record is in the center, the integrated online catalog represented by the second layer and highlighted to show authority control. The wide outer band is where the other functions reside, but all again, using that one bibliographic record.

The most interesting thing about this diagram is the triangle of use formed by the interaction between Public Services, Collection

DIAGRAM A

```
┌──────────────────┐
│ Materials ordered │
└──────────────────┘
         │
         ▼
┌──────────────────┐
│ Materials received│
└──────────────────┘
         │
         ▼
┌──────────────────┐          ┌──────────────────────┐
│                  │────────▶ │ Bibliographic records │
│ Materials        │          │ loaded into Gemini     │
│ cataloged        │          └──────────────────────┘
│                  │                     │
└──────────────────┘                     ▼
         │                    ┌──────────────────────┐
         ▼                    │ Bibliographic access  │
┌──────────────────┐          │ available to patron   │
│ Materials        │          │ in Gemini             │
│ processed        │          └──────────────────────┘
└──────────────────┘                     ▲
         │                                │
         ▼                    ┌──────────────────────────────┐
┌──────────────────┐          │ Interlibrary Loan materials   │
│ Materials        │◀───────▶ │ and bibliographic records     │
│ available        │          │ available both locally and    │
│ to patron        │          │ nationally                    │
└──────────────────┘          └──────────────────────────────┘
```

DIAGRAM B

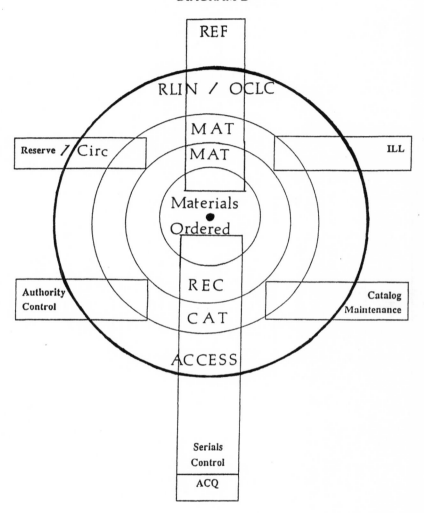

Development and Technical Services. Whichever way you turn the circle, the area of function is exactly the same. This is an equilateral triangle, with the sides and all three angles equal. No one division is more important than the other, there are no barriers, no standoffs, no walls.

DIAGRAM C
LIBRARY INFORMATION SYSTEM

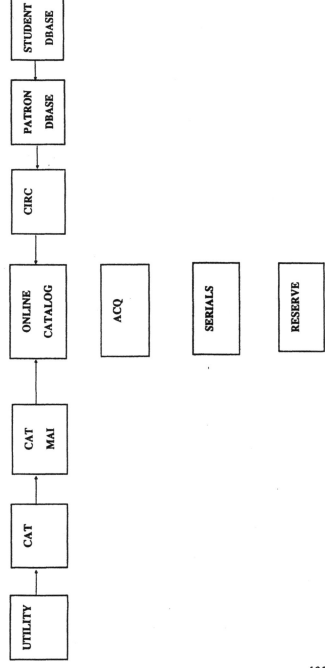

DIAGRAM D

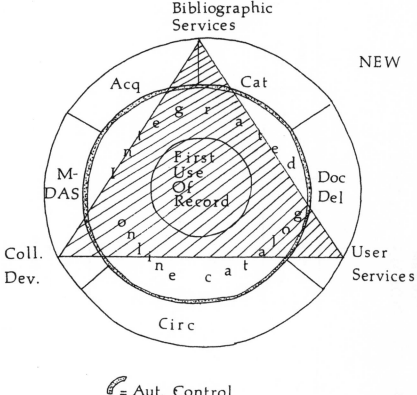

Bibliographic
Services

NEW

Acq   Cat

M-
DAS

Coll.
Dev.

First
Use
Of
Record

Doc
Del

User
Services

Circ

𝒢 = Aut. Control

⟁ = Access Interaction
(Golden Triangle)

THE NEW EQUATION

This is the working relationship that we are moving toward, created for the most part by the development of truly integrated library information systems. However, there are other factors working to create a supportive environment for this change. Fifteen years ago, the area of the library that was really familiar with automation—

usually in the form of an OCLC record—was Technical Services. This has changed. Reference librarians, having had an online catalog around for awhile, feel familiar with it. They have started to take ownership and are making improvements. Another factor is the advent of CD-ROMs as a reference tool. Many libraries have started to merge their mediated search or Computer Search Services staff with the regular reference staff, a sign that barriers are breaking down within the Reference Department as a whole. If the Reference Librarians were considered the elite of the library profession, the Computer Search Services librarians were the pinnacle. The Bibliographic Instruction librarians are also becoming more part of the department. There is a new breed of young, peppy B.I. people who love computers and who are delighted to be using their skills both in the library and elsewhere on campus.

Another important factor in creating a supportive environment for these changes is the migration from early online systems to second if not third generation systems. Reference Librarians are much more involved in that process than they were several years ago. As a result, the emphasis on the importance of patron access is increasing. This is also a result of patron feedback, as our faculty and students become more computer literate and demand more services.

One outcome of this interaction is the increased familiarity of Reference Librarians with MARC format—tagging, fixed fields and indicators are no longer the arcane terminology of an abstruse and cabalistic sect, but tools to assist the patron. Reference Librarians have to know the fields that Boolean and key word searches will be pulling from in order to best serve the user. Online systems have become sophisticated enough to provide reports of system usage which can aid catalogers in providing better bibliographic access. Reports can be generated on demand of unsuccessful searches.[13] In many cases, this will show typos, miskeying, etc., but can also show a need for new cross-references to be added by catalogers.

This familiarity with bibliographic records in machine readable form is strengthened with the new emphasis on Collection Development as the searcher of *the* record to be used. Many bibliographers also do reference work and the connections between the access points used to provide information and the access points used to pull out information are coming closer and closer. The thought processes used for both these functions can have very different results. However, with Collection Development/Reference being in at the establishment of the record, there is hope that the gap between the two will be narrowed considerably. Research has been done to show that full subject access is only provided with a combination of post and pre-coordinate subject vocabulary searches.[14]

TRANSCENDING BOUNDARIES

It is very difficult to be conducting "business as usual" whilst the profession and its major functionalities are redefining themselves. In order to think across boundaries and take advantage of interdependencies, to revitalize our profession, we must develop a mental flexibility which challenges all the old categories we have spent so many years with. In the field of higher education, and especially within our profession, it has become the fashion to sneer at the bottom line mentality of the business world, and the never-ending sequence of contra-indicatory management philosophies, that fill the pages of the management literature. We need to break down the barriers of our very own boxes and think imaginatively about matters of both form and substance.

As Rosabeth Moss Kantor said in a recent editorial in *Harvard Business Review*, "Innovations grow out of unexpected, surprising, and even irreverent mental connections. To develop them requires collaborations and adjustments by many parts of the organization. Entrepreneurial opportunities do not respect territories; they rarely present themselves to companies in the boxes established on the organizational chart. But the more rigid the walls between functions or between divisions, the less likely that people will venture out of their boxes to try something new."[15]

Only if we work harder at rethinking categories and transcending boundaries will we empower ourselves to serve our clients in a way more suited to the technology and the demands of the year 2000.

REFERENCES

1. Neal, James G. "And the Walls Came Tumblin' Down: Distributed Cataloging and the Public/Technical Services Relationship—the Public Services Per-

spective," *1984: Challenges to an Information Society.* Knowledge Industry Publications, 1984.

2. Altmann, Anna A. "The Academic Library of Tomorrow: Who Will Do What?" *Canadian Library Journal*, June 1988, pp. 147-152.

3. Gorman, Michael, "On Doing Away With Technical Services," *American Libraries*, 10, July/August 1979, p. 435.

4. Gorman, Michael, "The Ecumenical Library," *The Reference Librarian*, 10, Fall/Winter 1983, pp. 55-64.

5. Pastor, Amy, "Dual Function Librarianship: What Makes it Work?" This issue.

6. Gorman, Michael, "Reorganization at the University of Illinois-Urbana/Champaign Library: A Case Study," *Journal of Academic Librarianship*, 9: pp. 223-5, September 1983.

7. De Gennaro, Richard as reported in *Library Hotline*, v.xix, no. 49, p. 4.

8. Davenport, Sara, "The Blurring of Divisional Lines Between Technical and Public Services: An Emphasis on Access." This issue.

9. McCombs, Gillian M. "Public and Technical Services: The Hidden Dialectic," *RQ*, v. 28, no. 2, Winter 1988, pp. 141-145.

10. Kantor, Rosabeth Moss. "Thinking Across Boundaries," *Harvard Business Review*, v. 68, no. 6, Nov/Dec. 1990, pp. 9-10.

11. Op. Cit.

12. Niles, Judith. "Technical Services Reorganization For An Online Integrated Environment." *Cataloging & Classification Quarterly*, 9, no. 1: 11-17, 1988.

13. Innovative Interfaces Inc., *System Description* (documentation), Berkeley, CA, 1988, p. 14.

14. Markey, Karen. "Alphabetical Searching in an Online Catalog," Journal of Academic Librarianship, 14:353-60. January 1989.

15. Kantor, Rosabeth Moss, op. cit.

IV. NATIONAL
LIBRARY WIDE CONCERNS

Education for the Dual Role
Responsibilities
of an Access Services Librarian

Sheila S. Intner

SUMMARY. The change in attitude from acquisition to access requires a new kind of librarian. What are the skills needed by "access librarians?" What kind of leadership role will they play in library service? Are libraries ready for these changes? How can library-schools make a curriculum out of the skills needed for access and leadership? If properly prepared, new visions of access will come from librarians to lead the field into the twenty-first century.

One of the most critical trends in libraries has been the shift from the library-centered organization around "Public," "Technical," and "Administrative" services as the basic structural division to organizational structures based upon client-centered divisions such

Sheila S. Intner is Professor at Simmons College, Graduate School of Library and Information Science, Boston, MA 02115.

The author appreciates the assistance of Linda Watkins and Charlotte Hegyi, Simmons College Library Science Librarians, in preparation of this paper.

as language, subject, or audience groupings. These new divisions include distributed and integrated support functions, including technical processing, as well as distributed shelving of collections.[1]

It is not unusual for a library to shelve its science materials and the German literature materials in separate sections, or even separate buildings, while maintaining a central cataloging department that processes all of them, but it is less common to shelve the materials separately and also maintain two cataloging departments, one for science materials and one for German literature materials. The paradigm shift in organization, however, goes beyond this simplistic notion of distributed processing, to divide tasks according to the knowledge they require, i.e., knowledge of a professional nature or general knowledge. To continue with the example, the science and the German literature divisions would each have groups of librarians and support staff. In each division, the librarians would be assigned to do all the professional tasks required in the division, including planning, budgeting, training, programming, selection, cataloging, reader's advisory, and research services, etc. while the support staff would do all the work of a nonprofessional nature, such as data entry, file maintenance, labeling, shelving, etc. Each science librarian and German literature librarian might not do all eight types of professional tasks every day or week of the year, but they would be prepared to do them all and would typically do several at once, with the mix changing as needed throughout the year.

Is this, indeed, a paradigm shift? Catalogers who cover reference desks often are encountered in all sorts of libraries. Having bibliographers who spend a little time cataloging is not as common, but not entirely absent from the library scene. Why all the fuss?

Two elements in the current trend lead to new perceptions about dual role librarians, and both relate to access: (1) the goal of library leadership is no longer to acquire everything one's clients might conceivably want, but to gain access to it;[2] and, (2) professional functions are changing to become leadership functions directed toward these goals, and moving away from focusing solely on becoming expert in one or another of the parts of the process.[3] These two factors are explored in some depth in this paper, and a new paradigm for library education to prepare dual-role librarians is suggested to respond to them.

NOT ACQUISITION, BUT ACCESS

Some years ago, a survey of faculty perceptions of academic collection quality determined that the only criterion on which all respondents unanimously agreed was size: the bigger the collection, the better.[3.5] Clearly, chief executive officers of libraries today would like to acquire every publication they think their clients might want to use, were it possible to do so, just as they have always tried to do in the past. The difference now is that the cost of buying even a small portion of the nation's and the world's much larger information output has become an enormously expensive proposition. Even buying all of what libraries think they really need is a job that lies beyond their budgets, especially the budgets of general research libraries which, if they had their druthers, would feel justified in buying everything published everywhere on the grounds that scholars eventually will find a need for every item someday, even if there is no particular demand for all of them now.

The change in attitude toward acquiring everything needed for one's clients is the result of necessity, or, perhaps, of facing the reality that the old philosophy simply won't work in today's information environment — the environment of exponentially increasing information production. The old posture was untenable, so it had to be discarded and replaced with a new one that had some hope of working.

Librarians did not have to look very far to find a viable alternative. Libraries are perennially short of funds, and the tradition of sharing materials through interlibrary loan has been around for at least four or five centuries, since the Dominicans began preparing union lists of monastic holdings in the fifteenth century to accommodate studious friars at different locations. The notion of sharing materials, however, matured rapidly over the last thirty years with the development of library computing and its enormous power to build bibliographic databases and distribute them instantly to anyone possessing a properly programmed terminal and the right to use it.

Computerized bibliographic networks have given rise to a new environment — one in which failing to acquire something through purchase does not mean being unable to acquire it rapidly and easily. Computing has given new meaning to library resource sharing by supporting, first, instantaneous distribution of information about materials and, later, the materials themselves to a virtually infinite number of recipients regardless of their geographic locations. Nor has it stopped there. Computers continue to spur creation of newer and more sophisticated methods of acquiring materials, information, and knowledge.

What Is Access?

Access is one of those amorphous words that can mean almost anything the speaker or writer wants it to mean. In the non-library world of everyday living, access means availability, and it is used for that simple meaning by librarians generally to mean the availability of information. But availability is not identical with either possession or use, thus a general definition is not adequate for this analysis.

More specifically, in the jargon of catalog librarians, access means bibliographic access, or the provision of catalog records that can be searched by information seekers in place of the actual physical items. In the jargon of circulation librarians (and a great many library patrons), access means shelf access, the presence of open stacks to which library patrons can go freely to select whatever items they want. In the jargon of collection development librarians, access means the ability to find and obtain for their own patrons materials their libraries do not own and will not purchase, artfully combining the two previous definitions and augmenting them to form yet a third definition. The collection developer's definition of access involves, first, knowing an item exists, usually by means of a system of bibliographic access; second, determining who has shelf access to the item; and third, establishing contact with them and arranging for the right to use the item temporarily in some mutually agreeable way, perhaps by paying for the use or by promising to lend that library some other item wanted by its patrons in the future.

The collection developer's definition comes closest to the definition of access needed to understand the transition librarians have made and are making from being gatherers of collections and owners of documents to being providers of information. In fact, however, a subtle change in the definition has been taking place in the last several years as well, as access to information has begun to assume the position of a *right*, not merely an option.

The idea of having a right to use the bibliographic data in computerized networks has added an entirely new meaning to the word "access." One cannot exercise the right of access if one does not pay for it by subscribing or belonging to the network. And while the right of access is not limited solely to computerized information, it is the frequency with which charges are levied for it and the debate over whether such charges are fair or ethical that has engendered this new view of access. We hear librarian-politicians speak about the "right of access to information" in much the same way ordinary politicians speak of our inalienable human rights—the rights of all citizens of the United States to life, liberty, and the pursuit of happiness. "After all," the librarian-politicians reason, "how can one pursue happiness, life or liberty without information? If information is essential, then access to it also must be part of the fundamental rights guaranteed by our Constitution."

Are All Libraries Prepared for Access?

The metamorphosis from accumulators of knowledge to distributors of knowledge is a transition that still is in progress and has quite a way to go before librarians everywhere typically will perceive themselves in this new role and will have the wherewithal to accomplish its goals and objectives. Clearly, not all libraries are prepared for the change, even though it is far from a new one. The metamorphosis actually began in the United States more than 100 years ago, with the advent of the dictionary catalog, the periodical index, the provision of reader's advisory services, and other tools of information provision.

Before that time, which started during the mid- to latter-nineteenth century, using libraries meant knowing exactly what one wanted and where it was, while the library's job was to have it. A cataloging student once related an incident that illustrates the difference. It occurred when she was traveling abroad in Italy, visiting a famous monastery. Remembering that the monastery was known for its library, she asked where the library was and was told it was closed, but would be open the following day, at one o'clock. Brimming with excitement, she went to the proper room the following afternoon, and asked to see the catalog. The librarian, a stern-looking nun, asked her what book she wanted to look up.

"I don't know yet," said the student, "that is why I want to see the catalog."

"Our policy forbids patrons to see the catalog unless they are looking up a specific title," said the nun-librarian.

The student was speechless. She told the class, "I thought to myself, 'How could I tell her what I wanted to look up, without first seeing the catalog and finding out what they had?'" And she went on, "I was so surprised by the nun's reply that my mind went blank, and I couldn't think of any old title to use as an excuse to get her to produce the catalog." Eventually, after a lengthy explanation that she was an American library science student interested in examining the catalog for its own sake, the nun relented and bent the rules, permitting her to look at it briefly before the library closed for the day.

The librarian at the monastery was not a servant of the public, committed to disseminating knowledge and providing access to all interested parties who came to her door seeking information they needed or wanted. She was, instead, the guardian of the treasure of knowledge the monastery had accumulated. Her mandate was to allow items from the treasure to be used only by knowledgeable people — bona fide scholars — and only under strict conditions that would insure their safe return to their appointed locations within the library's closed stacks. These perspectives on librarianship were not atypical in earlier centuries and in other places. They represent the traditions from whence twentieth century American librarianship sprang, but we have adapted and, perhaps, mutated in fundamental ways.

Cutter, Dewey, Poole, and others in the United States did much to reshape and democratize the library's bibliographic infrastructure and make it accessible to the common citizen. Cutter recommended the dictionary catalog over the classified catalog popular in Europe, because being filed by the letters of the alphabet it could be used by any person who knew their ABC's. To use a classified catalog, one had to understand the organization of the scholarly disciplines, which is no trivial matter to a novice. Cutter went further and declared that the language of the subject catalog (something the nun-librarian, who dealt entirely with known items, would not need at all) should match the language of its users, preferring terms in common usage over technical jargon. Dewey's famous classification scheme was an overwhelming success, because it furnished browsable collections. If stacks are closed, who needs browsing? But, when they are open and library patrons can move freely among them to locate the books they want, then a browsable arrangement makes sense. Poole, father of periodical indexes, did for the periodical literature what Cutter did for library catalogs containing records for books.

These three pioneers opened up new avenues of access to the American library patron: Cutter opened bibliographical access to books through the library catalog, Poole opened bibliographical access to the contents of journals through the printed index, and Dewey opened shelf access to library holdings through the hierarchical subject arrangement of books. But all of them dealt with owned materials. The country was not ready for other kinds of access, then, not even for the notion of widespread resource sharing as we know it today.

Unfortunately, many twentieth century libraries still are struggling with the traditional access of Cutter, Dewey, and Poole. They are tied to their manual systems and their physical holdings. If they don't own something, it is likely to take weeks or months to find and obtain it. Their medium of communication is the mail, or, if they are lucky, the telephone. If a library has not joined the computer revolution, and if it has not become part of the network of regional, national and international networks, then its librarians are powerless to contemplate moving ahead to newer routes to access that depend on computers and telecommunications.

These libraries may share the same globe, but they are not part of the developing library-global-village. While they certainly are not ready to consider a paradigm shift in their perceptions of access, they nevertheless are competing with those that have. Feelings of dislocation, isolation, and frustration are likely to develop with increasing intensity in libraries tied to manual access to local holdings. The contrast between them and the libraries whose collections are enhanced by electronic document delivery systems is as far beyond simple circulation of owned items as star wars is beyond the musket.

What Skills Do Access Librarians Require?

The quick answer to this question is computer expertise, the ability to communicate, research and problem solving skills, the ability to take risks and the ability to train others. These skills are in addition to, not in place of, knowledge of information and how to find it, familiarity with one's institution and its people, and understanding of library systems and services.

As one might imagine, computer expertise is one of the skills access librarians now require. More than the ability to operate a computer, one must understand computer capabilities and design, and be able to analyze whether and how computing can be employed to bring about desired goals and objectives. The new access librarian must be sufficiently adaptable to face a new machine and be able to transfer what he or she knows about computing in general to gain mastery over it quickly, yet sufficiently humble to learn the new machine's capabilities from those who know, or by trial and error.

The new access librarian needs communication skills, including the twin abilities to express himself or herself clearly and to listen carefully to what others say. It is not enough to be able to talk easily to one's colleagues or patrons, one must be able to communicate one's needs and concerns to people outside those familiar groups, to experts from other disciplines, to funding agents inside and outside one's own institution as well as to understand the meaning of what they have to say.

An important new skill for access librarians is problem solving. Problem solving, which depends heavily on knowledge of research, includes the ability to investigate a problem in an objective manner, to make assumptions and devise hypotheses about the problem and to test their applicability, to weigh alternative strategies and outcomes to solve the problem, to recognize their advantages and disadvantages, costs and benefits, and then to select among them, based on a set of valid criteria pertaining to the situation. Problem solving is not easy, and even when it must be done quickly to meet a deadline, it cannot be done without thought and it must not be done carelessly. Librarians must guard against allowing personal biases to jaundice their objectivity and drive their decisions.

Since decision making is heavily dependent on data and data is never complete, there is always an element of risk involved. Librarians in general are not known for being great risk takers. On the contrary, librarians are known as a conservative lot, unwilling to contravene tradition and innovate, and access librarians are no exception. Moreover, it is understandable why librarians are reluctant to explore, to strike out on untrodden paths – there has been little reward for experimenting, even if one succeeds, and a great deal of negative fallout for those who dare to be different. The library establishment is not rooting for its pioneers. Instead, it prizes conformity, avoids teaching people how to calculate risks, fails to motivate them to try new things, and, when they do take a risk despite all this, raises barriers of all sorts to their progress. Negativity toward risk taking must be overcome, since access to information is far from being a well-established, cut-and-dried set of operations. Access to information is evolving rapidly, and depends on systems and situations that are changing equally rapidly. Playing effectively in the access game will depend, for one thing, on the librarian's ability to anticipate and take advantage of technological changes affecting information production and delivery as well as other equally challenging factors that he or she cannot control.

New access routes will involve more complex systems and procedures, and the ability to teach others how to use them will be part of the librarian's job. Training others takes many special skills, including knowledge of the subject, preparation of training methods and materials, delivery of the information, and evaluation of the results. Training one person at a time requires adapting one's training style to the learning style of the trainee, while training people in a group requires being able to speak well before a group of people and to manage the training group.

ACCESS AND LEADERSHIP

Access librarians, i.e., librarians whose job is to furnish access to information for clients, have a leadership role to play in library service. They are not unique or unusual in this respect, because in the future all specially-educated and trained librarians will be expected to play leadership roles in information service. But access librarians are responsible for a critical aspect of service, therefore they may expect to be highly visible, even pivotal in the library's success or failure to serve the public effectively.

Until now, very few librarians exercised any leadership functions in the course of their practice. They became catalogers, or bibliographers, or reader's advisors, and did most of their work alone, although they also might supervise a few support staff in carrying out nitty gritty operations connected with cataloging, collection development, and reference. Some of these librarians became department heads who supervised groups of catalogers, bibliographers, reader's advisors, etc., i.e., the library's middle managers. A few chose to avoid even a hint of managerial responsibility, turning down chances for middle management jobs, but most welcomed the opportunity to direct other librarians in performing library services, to rise above the ranks and move up the ladder toward fame and riches. A few of the middle managers were tapped for higher level administrative echelons, i.e., as assistant or associate administrators, and coordinated the work of the middle managers. Eventually, some of the assistants and associates became chief executive officers, i.e., library directors, deans, chief librarians, or what-have-you who coordinated the work of the assistants and associates. Rising to the top of the ladder and becoming CEOs, however, did not guarantee that these people were leaders. It merely guaranteed that they had full opportunities to become leaders, for, as CEOs, they had nothing holding them back from exercising leadership functions.

What Is Leadership?

From the foregoing description, it should be clear that leadership involves more than supervision or management. How shall we distinguish among these functions? Supervision, in my thesaurus, is a synonym for "oversight."[4] It means keeping track, looking after, or overseeing that a job progresses without errors and is performed properly. It has nothing to do with deciding what job should be done, and, in practice, it may have nothing to do with setting the parameters of the job.

Management, on the other hand, is a much stronger activity, according to the same thesaurus, akin to conducting, controlling, and directing.[5] To simplify a bit, it says that managing means manipulating others to achieve a response, or it may mean the action of one who is in authority and charged with handling the details of a business or one of its departments. Management also might mean leadership, but the two words are not identical. In practice, management carries responsibility for telling people what to do and controlling the way jobs are done as well as being accountable for the results. In contrast, leader is linked with "chief" and "master"; among the definitions of lead are "set," "fix," and "establish"; and the first synonyms for leading are "governing" and "ruling."[6] The activity of leadership appears to be as much stronger than management as management was over supervision. It carries in its definition the notion of setting goals and fixing the sights of the organization, i.e., deciding what to do, what jobs will be performed, and where the organization will go.

It is the third and strongest definition that should apply to the leadership of access services. Leadership is proactive, not reactive. It does not involve following the instructions of others, but taking others in the direction the leader wishes to go. It means making the big decisions, which managers and supervisors then will carry out.

Are All Libraries Ready for Leadership?

All libraries are not ready to go where no one has gone before, to paraphrase Star Trek's Captain Kirk. Rather, they are anxious or feel bound to continue (read, *follow*) traditions of service that have gone before them. Their librarians do not wish to "rock the boat," "make waves," or "shake things up," which is an understandable posture coming from people who have worked their way through large bureaucracies and who have succeeded by becoming excellent bureaucrats.

In bureaucracies, upper-level administrators are swift to rebuke lower-level administrators who do things in unorthodox ways, or who fail to march to the designated music, hearing and heeding, instead, a different beat. In those libraries where statistics measuring services rendered to the public in terms of the numbers of items circulated, interloaned, or used in-house are ignored, there are no points to be earned by increasing them. In particular, in those libraries where rewards are not tied to services rendered, expanding service is a labor of love, not a primary job responsibility. In such libraries, no one cares if fewer books were taken off the shelves, borrowed and read in carrels, dormitories, or offices. No one cares if more students were turned away from the reserve desk this month, because the single copy of a required reading for a huge first-year English class was not returned. No one cares if fewer books were obtained from other libraries this term, because the staff member in charge left and has not been replaced. No one counts and no one cares if graduate students doing doctoral research are having a difficult time obtaining copies of other institutions' dissertations, because the charges are prohibitive. And no one cares if the online search service had fewer customers this year, because charges for the service were instituted in part to discourage overwhelming demand for the service and for the materials in the bibliographies it produced that were not owned by the library and had to be interloaned. In such a setting, if a librarian tries to institute policies and procedures to render more service to the public in terms of books used, interloans filled, dissertations borrowed, and online searches performed, who will reward them? Certainly not their superiors.

What kinds of measures are the measures of success named above? They are measures of access. They count the number of times library clients obtained physical access to wanted materials by the several routes with which most librarians currently are familiar, namely, ordinary loans, reserve loans, and interlibrary loans. They also count the number of times library clients obtained bibliographic access, and, possibly, physical access through electronic databases. Yet librarians in those institutions do not seem to worry that it is a serious problem when measures of access don't count.

How is success measured in libraries that do not measure it by services rendered? It tends to be measured by the size of the collections, the size of the budget, the size of the staff, and, perhaps, the numbers of items ordered, cataloged, etc. One might argue that the larger the collections, budgets, etc., the greater the potential for service to be rendered, and that is true. In fact, it is our general assumption that more collection means more service. But such counts fail to examine service at all, substituting for it measurements that can grow even when real service is shrinking.

Considering the nature of library organization, i.e., bureaucracy, and the criteria by which success seems to be measured, i.e., collection-centered numbers, not services rendered, the wonder is that librarianship has produced any leaders with vital interests in access at all, not that it has failed to produce enough of them.

What Skills Do Leaders Require?

The simple answer to this question is imagination, confidence, a vision of what he or she wants to be accomplished, and the ability to inspire others to accept that vision and follow it.

Imagination, one might say, is not a skill, but a personal characteristic that is part of one's genetic inheritance. That might be true, yet one cannot help but wonder whether the exercise of imagination is not something that can be nurtured and developed, if not actually taught. Conversely, perhaps the exercise of imagination is a quality that can be crushed by outside forces that declare it a liability. Thus, the environmental influences on people may serve to enhance or diminish their natural exercise of imagination. Given the tiny number of truly imaginative people that we recognize in our adult society, either there are very, very few of them to begin with, or elements in our environment dampen the exercise of imagination in those who have it.

Confidence, on the other hand, is something many believe is learned from achieving success, and, therefore, can be taught. The confident person believes in his or her ability to win whatever prize is sought. If one does not possess this personal power of positive thinking, one can acquire it by setting small goals, reaching them, and building on those successes by setting increasingly ambitious goals. Eventually, one will become confident in one's ability to succeed, provided, of course, one also has worked at developing the skills needed, including, for example, speaking and writing skills, listening skills, mathematical skills, athletic skills, etc.

That leadership requires a vision of where to go or what to accomplish is axiomatic. Yet one may assume a position of leadership without having such a vision, and in that case, one fails to lead even though given the potential and the power. It seems to this author that those in positions of leadership in libraries often have disappointed, because they did not have command of this skill. They may have excelled at organizing people and getting things done, they may have produced splendid successes when asked to manage a budget, build a building, or deal with personnel issues. But, when left to their own devices to think up future goals, they looked backward or sideward, not forward. The problem may be that one cannot expect to see a great many familiar things when one looks forward, and the unknown is hazy and difficult to recognize as well as frightening and uncertain. Nevertheless, it seems clear that part of leadership is exercising the skill of seeing into the future and deciding what it contains and what will be applauded as appropriate goals and objectives by the rest of the field, when the future has become the present and they have caught up to the leader.

The final leadership skill is the ability to inspire others with one's vision and to persuade them to follow one's lead. One who leads only himself or herself isn't much of a leader; one cannot be a leader without followers. In this respect, leadership is quite similar to supervision and management. There must be at least one person other than one's self in order to be a supervisor; and managers must accomplish their goals and objectives through the efforts of the people they manage. Leaders do something more than direct and control their followers, however. Leaders describe what the future will be and persuade their followers to believe in it. This motivates followers to accept the leader's goals and objectives and make them their own. The difference may seem very small, but it is truly enormous.

EDUCATION FOR THE NEW PARADIGM

The stated purpose of this article was to explore the education that will be needed for access librarians of the future. Access librarians of the future are likely to differ from today's "circulation" librarian or "document delivery" librarian in several respects. First and most important, they are likely to be expected to fill a dual role that includes both technical and public service knowledge and responsibilities, since it now is clear that both types of service are based on bibliographic expertise. Access librarians will be integrated librarians.

Second, temporary access to materials on an as-needed basis is beginning to gain favor as a method of serving the public in place of or equivalent to the ownership of materials. One reason temporary access strategies have assumed respectability is that they are a realistic response to the impossibility of buying all the publications a library's clients might need. Another is that temporary access is a natural extension of the way a computer-based society functions. One accesses the material one needs from the world's knowledge database, uses it, perhaps even stores it for a while, then deletes it when the need ends. Should one need that same piece of information again, it can be accessed again, just as easily. Material in the world knowledge database is always available and easily manipulated. One only needs to have access to the database. Thus, future modes of access will demand a different perspective and a different value system for access librarians than those of the own-it-or-forget-it library of the past did.

A third change for future access librarians will be the emphasis placed on leadership as a professional responsibility. Truly professional librarians need not fear being replaced either by lower paid clerical personnel or by computers, because leadership requires a finely honed human attribute — the ability to envision something new. Truly professional access librarians of the future are not going to be concerned whether Mr. X and Ms. Y paid their last dollar's worth of fines, or whether Dr. Z is a member of the full-time resident faculty or merely a visiting adjunct from Oshkosh. The big decision of the day will not be to excuse Mr. X's and Ms. Y's fines and allow them to take out books, or to bend the rules and allow Dr. Z to make an interlibrary loan request. Thus far, the skills needed for access and for leadership have been explored. They include computer expertise, the ability to communicate, research and problem solving skills, risk-taking ability, the ability to train others, imagination, confidence, a vision of what he or she wants to be accomplished, and the ability to inspire others to accept that vision and follow it. How can we make a curriculum out of these?

The New Mission of Library Education

The mission of library education has evolved in the little more than a century since Dewey started Columbia University's School of Library Service from training people to run a library to preparing them for their first jobs as neophyte catalogers, bibliographers, reader's advisers, or administrators. A mission for programs of library education consistent with the new paradigm will necessarily revert to preparing people to run libraries, but not solely in a mechanical or technical sense. As Francis Miksa demonstrated with regard to the subject of cataloging, "Cataloging education began with a focus on bibliographic system making as a total concept. Over the decades, however, this sense of cataloging has been narrowed in regularly named cataloging courses to the idea of cataloging as the preparation of entries. With that narrowing, however, new emphases have arisen, specifically, cataloging as management and cataloging theory. More recently, the combination of information retrieval thinking and new powerful technologies has brought back the notion of cataloging as the entire process of making bibliographic systems."[7] As Miksa points out, management and research have risen in importance generally in library education. These elements, combined with concomitant changes in thinking and potential brought about by computing and information science theory, have provided the opportunity for library practice to go back to what it once was, i.e., making a library. For access librarians, the change will be dramatic, since, for the last several decades, access has meant the dreary stamping of due dates, the petty collection of pennies for overdue books, and the tedious filling in of interlibrary loan forms. In place of these dull, repetitive, clerical tasks, access librarians are regaining their place in the bibliographic firmament along with the opportunity to make whole access systems.

Translating the New Skills into Curriculum

The most critical body of curriculum is the core that all students are required to share, comprising the basic body of principles that all librarians are expected to use in practice. At this point, the core curriculum in many library schools consists of four or five offerings such as an introductory survey of the field, beginning cataloging, beginning reference, collection development, and beginning management. Occasionally, other courses are included, also, e.g., basic research methods or introduction to information science. Certainly the research methods course needs to be mandated everywhere, and backed up with a preparation in modern statistical applications that students should have had prior to entering the graduate program. To these we need to add courses in oral and written communication for librarians, interpersonal relations, problem analysis and solution, risk analysis, and training methods. A mentoring program for students that matches each one with seasoned practitioners and/or educators should have as one of its goals to help build confidence through the accomplishment of such practical simulations as writing a grant proposal, writing and defending a budget, setting program goals, designing a request for proposal from a vendor, negotiating a contract, and writing an annual report.

The traditional core courses of cataloging, reference, and collection development, which are the primary functional activities based on bibliographic systems, including information storage, retrieval, and use, should be integrated into a different set of courses that first study the principles of bibliographic systems, and then study their applications in library settings. Preparation for becoming an access librarian would be embodied in these courses, and enhanced, perhaps, by an advanced level course covering specific types of access problems and issues.

A one-year graduate program will barely cover this larger core, but a two-year program would accommodate it in one year, with room for a selection of advanced level specialty courses in the second. At a minimum, one-year programs should provide every graduate with the augmented core curriculum, and should insure that knowledge about computer-based applications appropriate to the subject is included in every course. Students who wish to specialize in a type of library (academic, corporate, public, school, state, etc.), type of subject (medicine, law, art, film, music, etc.), or type of audience (children, youth, adults, senior citizens, non-English speaking, etc.) might be given the opportunity to take a group of advanced level courses and receive a certificate of specialization beyond the master's degree. Those library education programs already extended to two years might consider adopting the larger core in addition to their existing curricula, adding the mentor program, and giving their graduates a certificate of specialization in addition to the master's degree.

An Optimal Mix of Theory and Practice

As is obvious from the suggested curriculum in the previous section, a mix of theory and practice is appropriate to preparation of all librarians, as well as access librarians. Core courses should focus primarily on teaching principles (i.e., theory), with examples and illustrations from practice. No one will take the time or think it necessary to teach principles to practicing librarians, even new ones. One is supposed to come to practice with the principles already part of one's professional knowledge base, and it is the library school that must provide the groundwork. As A. J. Anderson has remarked, there is a fundamental difference between studying management (or anything else) as a discipline and studying how to perform its specific tasks.[8] Understanding the principles that underlie management activities and becoming familiar with the management literature, etc., is part of the curriculum of a theory-based course, not a practice-oriented one.

The mentor program is singled out as a means of providing practical applications of the principles learned in the core, e.g., negotiating a contract exercises communication skills, interpersonal relations, persuasion, and risk analysis, writing a grant proposal exercises writing skills, goal-setting, problem analysis, etc. Another strategy to furnish practical experience, and simultaneously fund a second year of library education for students of one-year programs is to place them in 3/4 time jobs while they continue taking courses. For access librarians, the mentor program might focus on budgeting, negotiating, proposal-writing, etc., for modes of access to information; while the 3/4 time apprenticeship might be as an assistant administrator in the access office of a library.

CONCLUSIONS

At the moment, in most libraries, access still consists of lending owned materials (circulation) or borrowing them from another library (interlibrary loan). Computer-based systems have speeded up the process of borrowing materials from sources outside the library beyond anything librarians might have hoped for before computing, but it still is the same process. Computer applications also have opened up larger bodies of bibliographic data for use in libraries and speeded up the process by which they are accumulated and delivered. They are beginning to supply the full text of documents represented by the bibliographic data as well (document delivery). Even these, however, are familiar processes, albeit with added bells and whistles. We still await the far-reaching innovations in access to information that new and emerging technologies can support.[9] Such new visions of access will come from librarians who are prepared, in the manner outlined above, to lead the field into the twenty-first century.

REFERENCES

1. See, for example, D. Kaye Gapen's description of such changes at the University of Wisconsin in "Transition and Change: Technical Services at the Center," Library Resources & Technical Services 33:285-96, or Maureen Sullivan's description of the new organizational structures at Yale University in her contribution to Cataloging, the Professional Development Cycle, Sheila S. Intner and Janet Swan Hill, eds. (Westport, CT: Greenwood Press, in press).

2. A fine description of the changes occurring in the focus of university research libraries may be found in Patricia Battin, "The Library: Centre of the Restructured University," Scholarly Publishing 17:255-67 (April 1986); see also Sheila S. Intner, "Differences between Access vs. Ownership," Technicalities 9:5-8 (Sept. 1989).

3. Some discussions of this trend may be found in Online Catalogs, Online Reference. Converging Trends, Proceedings of a Library and Information Technology Association Pre-conference Institute, June 23-24, 1981, Los Angeles, Brian Aveney and Brett Butler, eds. (Chicago: American Library Association, 1984).

3.5. F. W. Lancaster, If You Want To Evaluate Your Library . . . (Urbana: University of Illinois Graduate School of Library and Information Science, 1988), p. 20.

4. Webster's New Dictionary of Synonyms (Springfield, MA: G & C Merriam, 1973), p. 800.

5. Ibid., p. 520, 174.

6. Ibid., p. 489-90.

7. Francis Miksa, "Cataloging Education in the Library and Information Science Curriculum," in Recruiting, Educating, and Training Cataloging Librarians. Solving the Problems, Sheila S. Intner and Janet Swan Hill, eds. (Westport, CT: Greenwood Press, 1989), p. 291-92.

8. Conversations between the author and A. J. Anderson during the 1988-89 academic year, when he and the author served on a Simmons College Graduate School of Library and Information Science faculty committee to study the core curriculum.

9. For a glance at trends in circulation services, see Ryoko Toyama's two broad surveys of the literature: "The Year's Work in Circulation Control, 1987," and "The Year's Work in Circulation Control, 1988," Library Resources & Technical Services 32 (Oct. 1988):387-90 and 33 (Oct. 1989):331-34, respectively.

A United Professional Cadre

Allen B. Veaner

SUMMARY. The author holds that the time has come to abandon the still dominant nineteenth-century industrial organization and management models in librarianship and reunify the profession in preparation for the management challenges of the twenty-first century.

Although birth, growth, and death are ever cyclic in the living world, when it comes to human institutions, history does not necessarily repeat itself. Within our lifetimes we have seen the demise of many seemingly durable establishments: governments, businesses, and other major social organizations. Within one generation we have seen views of new library technology evolve from disbelief to scepticism, from doubt to distaste, from disdain to enthusiasm, and from enthusiasm to necessity. It would be perfect if our current attitudes towards new technology strengthened our profession to the point where politicians and the public would at last concede what we have known for centuries: that information, knowledge and their stewardship are the keys to wealth and human advancement. How comforting if some of the old familiar proverbs — brains count for more than brawn, the pen is mightier than the sword — actually dominated decision-making in the arena of public policy.

A CRITICAL TIME FOR THE PROFESSION

But in human affairs correct timing is vital. Successful space exploration requires precise launch windows — conveniently unique conjunctions of stars and planets to assure that spacecraft reach their targets; medical treatment must reach the patient within a certain

Allen B. Veaner is the principal of Allen B. Veaner Associates, 45 Inglewood Drive, Toronto, Ontario, M4T 1G9, Canada.

critical time; carbon dioxide production must be reduced before there is a runaway greenhouse effect, and so on. Could it be argued that librarianship, driven by technological change, is fast approaching a critical time that may determine its survival as a service and institution? Vannevar Bush's almost half century old Memex proposal, once seen as a semi-comic Buck Rogers fantasy, seems remarkably close to realization: it is almost within the power of modern technology—though not yet of economics—to put into the hands of an individual massive private libraries covering virtually any subject and all media. Does this mean that the library as we know it may soon no longer be a social necessity?

Without organization and effective means of retrieval, no Memex or similar device can help the information seeker. Anyone who ever purchased a massive microform collection or body of computer tapes not provided with bibliographic access knows the maddening frustration users experience when they confront masses of unorganized, inaccessible data. Seasoned librarians, indexers, and other information professionals are keenly aware that simple possession of a large collection of material—without organization and access—is meaningless, a point often overlooked by enthusiasts of the technological fix. Even though the genetic code transmits all the information necessary to construct a working human being, no human has yet figured out how to turn the information we create and record into efficient, self-organizing automata. Mere storage capacity and processing speeds of many millions of instructions per second do not, by themselves, put information into the hands of the users. But the purveyors of hardware and software keep trying to convince librarians, end users and administrators that the solution to the public's information retrieval problem lies in the purchase—at regular, almost predictable intervals—of ever more complex and expensive apparatus. Why? Because, in part, belief in the technological imperative contributes to the confusion between possession of informational materials and access systems.

COLLECTIONS VERSUS ACCESS

Where did this Berlin wall dividing possession from access come from in the first place? Well, the answer to this question is quite straightforward: when industrial methods were grafted onto librarianship during the 1920s, our profession institutionalized its functional differences into a structure of separate cadres — public services and technical services — to manage differing aspects of what in pre-industrial times was really an integrated service system. By industrializing librarianship, we transformed its milieu into a kind of bibliographic factory fragmented by function — a milieu now nearly dysfunctional.

How can we respond to this damaging bifurcation? First, we can acknowledge that the "stuff" of librarianship is not and never has been books, manuscripts, films, sound recordings, digitized data, or any other manufactured product of the publishing industry. Nor has the "stuff" of librarianship been hardware — whether in the form of a card catalogue, book stacks, a building, a photocopier, or a computer terminal. Essential as those things are, they are merely so much ink, paper, steel, silicon, stone, or other industrial material. Nor has true librarianship ever been the mere implementation of fixed rules and procedures. I have argued elsewhere, and I continue to assert, that librarianship is human beings serving other human beings' research and informational needs. The prime feature of our profession is its members' mental and intellectual activity and their inter-action with their clients — a form of dynamic software far more powerful, flexible and responsive than anything on diskettes. True librarianship is not a body of knowledge or set of skills, but a gestalt of attitudes, talents, dedication, intelligence, education, challenge, opportunity, and responsibility.

PRIORITIES FOR THE FUTURE

Now rapid technological and social change have brought us to that critical moment when old organizational paradigms no longer apply. Our first priority is to *communicate effectively* to our sponsors that we are in an ideal position to help those who administer public policy, because our work focuses on complex mental and heuristic processes that are intangible, unpredictable, unexpected, and unseen — precisely the focus of modern leadership responsibility in all sectors. Our second priority is to reassemble our own Humpty Dumpty. But as long as we remain split into warring factions it will be relatively easy for the hardware-oriented sector to convince governments, hospitals, schools, business, and others —

perhaps even the professoriate—that they have ready-made solutions to the complex problems that baffle humanity. Who will be the "knowledge navigators" of the future? Only the members of a unified profession. Only a united professional cadre, working in a collegial spirit, can seize the critical moment to redesign itself as a responsive new instrument capable of dealing with a constantly changing world and the competitive challenge of the for profit information sector.

From Document Delivery
to Information Access:
Convergence at the National Level

Thomas J. Galvin

SUMMARY. The American Library Association's program priorities since 1977 have increasingly centered on redefining the mission of the library in a broader context of total information access. Access has been addressed by the Association in relation to national information policy.

The Association's response to the work of its Commission on Freedom and Equality of Access to Information illustrates the difficulties that arise when member-governed organizations consider information policy options in public forums. Such debates may challenge fundamental professional values. The need to reexamine policy positions can conflict with the importance of maintaining a consistent public advocacy stance.

ALA has identified access as its highest priority and has begun enumerating characteristics of adequacy in the information access environment. There is little indication that the ALA organizational structure itself, however, yet reflects the transition from document delivery to information access.

In 1981, a study of the future role of the Los Angeles Public Library by the Arthur D. Little, Inc. consulting firm predicted that "between now and the year 2000, the idea of a 'library' as defined by LOCATION or PLACE will continue to give way at an accelerating pace to the idea of a library . . . as ACCESS NETWORKS."[1] More recently, in a 1989 paper on the character of the large research

Thomas J. Galvin is Director of the PhD Program in Information Science and Policy at the University at Albany, SUNY, 135 Western Avenue, Albany, NY 12222. He is Past-President and former Executive Director of the American Library Association.

library in the year 2020, seven participants in a conference for alumni of UCLA's Senior Fellows leadership development program assert that "the value of a library will not be measured by the size, depth or breadth of the collections owned, but rather by its ability to provide access to information in all formats."[2]

Implicit in such predictions as these is a fundamental redefinition and expansion of the role of the library from a relatively static physical entity concerned primarily with acquiring, organizing and making available locally-held information resources to a dynamic instrumentality for linking users with a total universe of information in the full range of both traditional and electronic formats. Such a far-reaching reconceptualization of the library's mission has potentially profound implications for the content and character of the professional staff assignment and for the organizational structures of libraries. In particular, the traditionally separate and distinct functions of reference and cataloging may increasingly come to converge around the concepts of information access and information delivery.

ACCESS AND THE AMERICAN LIBRARY ASSOCIATION

Professional societies in the library and information field tend to mirror the values, goals and structures of the communities of professionals whom they seek to serve. The American Library Association is the oldest and largest voluntary personal membership organization in the information field, with a current membership of approximately 50,000 individuals, institutions and organizations. Is there evidence that information access, broadly defined, has emerged as a major priority in the ALA program? Are there any signs of convergence in the Association's structure between technical and public service interests?

Over the past dozen years, access has indeed become increasingly prominent in the definition of ALA's organizational mission. Historically, ALA has had long-standing concerns for specific aspects of information access and information equity, notably in the domain of intellectual freedom, characterized by consistent, vigorous opposition to censorship and advocacy for First Amendment rights. More recently, public access to government information, the growth of fee-based information services, print and information literacy have become high profile items on the Association's action agenda. Increasingly, access-related issues have come to be viewed within the Association in the broader context of national information policy. A historically narrow Association focus on the library as an institution has begun to be tempered to some extent by a more holistic view of a larger, more diverse information universe.

Eric Moon, long an articulate public advocate for information equity, identified national information policy as the central theme for his ALA Presidential year in 1977-78. Two years later, the author of this paper, during his ALA Presidential term, convened an invitational seminar for twenty-eight national leaders from government, industry, communications, publishing, education and librarianship to begin to formulate "An Information Agenda for the 1980's." In the published summary of that event, Editor Carlton C. Rochell characterized "access" as "perhaps the most crucial issue for an information-based society."[3]

The 1980 ALA seminar made clear that the concept of information access required redefinition and expansion as a consequence of technological change, rising user expectations, the emergence of the private sector information industry and the diminishing role of government in direct support of the provision of library and information services to the public. "The dilemma," was characterized by William O. Baker, then Chairman of the board of Bell Telephone Laboratories and a participant in the seminar, as "how to enhance the capability of the user, at a time when demand on capability has exploded and the exercise of capability seems to be seriously deteriorating."[4]

THE LACY COMMISSION

As a follow-up to the 1980 seminar, in 1983 Carol Nemeyer, former Associate Librarian of Congress, created a Commission on Freedom and Equality of Access to Information as a principal programmatic activity of her term as ALA President. Chaired by Dan Lacy, former Senior Vice President of McGraw-Hill Inc., and consequently commonly referred to as the "Lacy Commission," this group comprised seventeen prominent individuals, only five of whom were drawn from the ranks of the library community. The remaining members of the Commission included representatives of authors, publishers, the learned societies, the media, communications and the information industry.

Over a two year period, the Commission sought to address five fundamental questions of information and public policy:

1. Have public authorities—federal, state, and local—themselves attempted to deny or limit access?
2. Does the technology of the newer media tend to broaden or to narrow access?
3. Does the economic organization of the newer media give private owners, as gatekeepers, a power to deny or limit access?
4. Are there significant barriers that limit the access of individuals to the information they need, even though it is available through the media?
5. Who should pay the costs of communication and how does that affect access? [5]

The scope of the Commission's investigation and analysis of these issues affirmed the need for the library community to place greater emphasis on pursuing its traditional educational and service goals in the larger context of a coordinated national information policy agenda.

The Lacy Commission's report considered an exceptionally broad range of information policy concerns, including telecommunications and broadcasting, libel, access to government information, censorship and the social impact of new technology. The Commission offered twenty-four action recommendations relating to these and other policy issues. The report sparked significant controversy within the Association's elected leadership, because several of its recommendations appeared to call into question, to contradict, or to compromise longstanding public policy positions of ALA. In particular, the Commission's comments and proposals on broadcast deregulation, on the expanding role of the private, for-profit sector in the dissemination of Federal government information and on the imposition of user fees as a method for achieving equitable access to information in electronic formats provoked intense public criticism from groups within the Association.

The highly contentious character of the ALA's Council's debate on the Commission's report exemplified an endemic problem that can arise when organizations such as ALA try to consider possible new policy options in public forums. It can be very difficult to sustain constructive dialogue on complex policy issues in which a vocal, articulate sector of the membership has a large emotional investment. Any effort to reexamine such issues dispassionately in light of what some perceive to be changing circumstances is likely to be regarded by others as a compromise of basic principles and a threat to fundamental professional values.

FEE OR FREE?

The controversial issue of user fees in libraries is an excellent case in point. Over the past decade, as libraries have tried to respond to the demand for technological enhancements in a climate of level or declining financial support, some of the costs of making new technology available have increasingly had to be borne directly by users through fees for such services as on-line searching. ALA policy flatly asserts "that the charging of fees and levies for information services, including those services using the latest information technology, is discriminatory in publicly supported institutions. . . ."[6]

The rationale for such a seemingly absolutist stance is based in the deep philosophic commitment of both ALA and the larger library community to equity and equality of service for *all* library users and to the obligation of government to finance high quality library service for all from public funds. Some ALA members believe that, as the leading organizational advocate for access and equity in information services, the Association ought not engage in public debate of proposals which might imply a possible willingness to compromise these fundamental principles and values. In its most extreme form, this view even calls into question the appropriateness of ALA's gathering information on the current practices of publicly funded libraries in obtaining a portion of their revenues from non-tax sources, since such data might appear to lend legitimacy to user fees as an income-generating mechanism for libraries. In essence, as illustrated by the intensity of the negative response to the Lacy Commission's suggestion that fees imposed on heavy users of on-line services might be appropriate in some circumstances, the user fee issue has become virtually non-debatable within the American Library Association.

THE COORDINATING COMMITTEE ON FREEDOM AND EQUALITY OF ACCESS TO INFORMATION

Although it engendered considerable divisiveness in the ALA Council, the Association's highest policy-making body, at the time it was initially received and considered, the Lacy Commission report, in retrospect, did help to direct continuing member attention to a broader agenda of access related policy issues. In addition, the report identified some important aspects of information access, such as support for public broadcasting, on which the Association had, up to that point, not developed a policy stance. A special committee was subsequently established to address implementation issues. That Committee, in turn, prompted several ALA units to give a higher priority to access matters, and led to a recognition of the cross-cutting character of complex policy questions. Consequently, a more permanent Coordinating Committee on Freedom and Equality of Access to Information was established in January 1989.

The new committee was charged:

> to facilitate the development and maintenance of a comprehensive set of information access policies for the American Library Association in cooperation with all Association units; to draw together key persons within the Association to focus on access issues; to monitor access activities outside ALA which are of interest to the Association; to facilitate communications among ALA units on access issues and suggest areas where activity and/or coordination is required within the Association; to aggressively support and, when needed, develop coalitions to further ALA policies on access; to identify needed research on access issues and follow through, to advise ALA Council and Executive Board on programs, policies and priorities in those areas of access not assigned to any other Council committee.[7]

This Committee's lengthy and awesome charge illustrates some of the problems that a complex, highly-fragmented organization like ALA encounters when it seeks to address access-related issues. ALA must parcel its agenda out to a myriad of divisions, round tables, boards and committees and then try to draw firm boundaries among their respective domains, simply for the sake of order and to avoid inconsistency and duplication of effort. Some specific aspects of information access raised by the Lacy Commission did not match any logical box on the Association's organizational chart, while others appeared to fall within the charge of more than one group. Some coordinating mechanism becomes essential in order to assure that important issues do not simply "fall through the organizational cracks."

The 1980 special colloquium, the 1986 Lacy Commission Report and its follow-up mechanisms all served to highlight "access" as ALA's most urgent priority concern. Consequently, it is not surprising that, in 1986, when the Association promulgated a new statement of its Mission, Priority Areas, and Goals, access was presented as the first of ALA's "overarching priorities."[8] In a very real sense, the five priority areas that follow access in this revised strategic planning document — legislation and funding, intellectual freedom, public awareness, personnel resources, library services, development and technology — may be regarded as either aspects of information access or as instrumentalities for achieving information equity.

The American Library Association, as a consequence of a more than a decade of high-profile activity, has identified information access as a central focus of Association-wide concern and has created at least one new organizational structure to address larger access-related policy issues. Yet the Constitution of ALA continues to express the Association's purpose in considerably narrower terms as the promotion of "library service and librarianship." This dichotomy is reflected, in turn, in the definition of the Association's legislative action agenda.

CATCH 22 FOR ALA

One dilemma for ALA is whether to spread its limited resources in the legislative and governmental relations arenas across a very broad spectrum of information policy issues. Some of these, like computer security or transborder data flows, appear to many ALA members to be only marginally related to the domain of librarianship. Alternatively, the Association can opt to concentrate its organizational forces and seek to maximize its impact on the more limited set of information policy matters, such as categorical aid to libraries, intellectual freedom and access to government information, on which it has established substantial organizational credibility over time. The more ALA's legislative program appears to depart from what has traditionally been regarded as the "library agenda," the more difficult it can become to sustain a broad base of member interest and support. Yet it is increasingly evident that libraries and library services, no matter how inclusively the latter may ultimately come to be defined, constitute only one element, albeit a critical one, in the mosaic of total information access. In short, for professional societies, just as for individual libraries, the matter of defining and refining organizational priorities becomes much more complex in a "total information access" environment.

Having identified "access" as its principal objective, the Association next faced the challenge of defining that concept in operational terms. Some initial progress has been made in that direction in the context of the ALA strategic planning process itself. Under the rubric of "access," seven organizational goals are specified, providing a partial enumeration of what might be termed characteristics of adequacy in the information access environment. These goals postulate a climate of universal information equity in which all have equal access to library and information services, bibliographic instruction is generally available, government information is readily accessible, library collections provide access to the total body of recorded knowledge, bibliographic organization facilitates, rather than impedes, access, library use is high and user fees do not constitute a barrier to information.[9]

The Association has also recognized and responded to the need to begin to develop basic indicators of the current state of information access for the nation. *America's Libraries: New Views*, a publication initiated in 1988 with grant support from OCLC Inc., will provide benchmark statistical data at periodic intervals. It is intended to enable both information professionals and citizen opinion leaders to assess national trends in such key areas as levels of library use and financial support.[10]

CONCLUSIONS

In summary, there is significant evidence that ALA has sought to come to terms with the broader definition of information access that is implicit in the transition from document delivery. At the national level, efforts to reformulate the mission and role of libraries in this more expansive context have produced many of the same kinds of tensions, conflicts and uncertainties as occur when these issues are considered at the level of the local library.

The concept of "information access" as a social and professional goal remains somewhat amorphous and as yet only partially defined by the profession. Additional criteria for adequate and effective access remain to be specified. It is perhaps time for the Association to set about creating a new "Library and Information Services Bill of Rights" that would enumerate more fully and in some greater detail the kind and level of information services that should be universally available through libraries in an electronic information age.

It is perhaps also time to consider the extent to which the divisional structure of the Association may help to perpetuate the more traditional view of the library as an entity comprised of separate and distinct functional activities concerned with the acquisition, organization or dissemination of documents. The existence of type-of-activity divisions within the Association, each with its own dues structure and discrete domain of policy responsibility, probably tends to encourage insularity. As the Association's experience in trying to allocate responsibility for addressing some of the Lacy Commission recommendations suggests, the ALA divisional structure also serves to complicate identification and consideration of larger access-related issues that cut across functional specializations.

In general, there is little evidence, up to this point, that the nation's largest professional organization in the library and information field has yet begun to recognize the possible implications for its own organizational structure of a potential convergence between technical and public service functions in libraries. Indeed, given the well documented tendency of bureaucracies to become self-perpetuating and the historic proclivity of the library profession to fragment

itself organizationally by type of library and by functional specialization, any restructuring of ALA's functional divisions seems more
likely to follow well behind, rather than to lead, a comparable restructuring of library staffs at the local level.

REFERENCES

1. Arthur D. Little, Inc., *The Los Angeles Public Library In the Information
Age* (Boston, November 1981), III-6.
2. Anne Woodsworth and others, "The Model Research Library: Planning
for the Future," *Journal of Academic Librarianship*, 15 (July, 1989), 134.
3. Carlton C. Rochell, ed., *An Information Agenda for the 1980s: Proceedings of a Colloquium June 17-18, 1980* (Chicago: American Library Association,
1981), p. 6.
4. Rochell, p. 10.
5. Commission on Freedom and Equality of Access to Information, *Freedom
and Equality of Access to Information: A Report to the American Library Association* (Chicago: American Library Association, 1986) p. 3.
6. American Library Association, "Free Access to Information," *ALA
Handbook of Organization, 1989-90* (Chicago: American Library Association,
1989), p. 240.
7. *ALA Handbook . . . 1989-90*, p. 9.
8. American Library Association, "Mission, Priority Areas, Goals," *ALA
Handbook . . . 1989-90*, p. 222.
9. Ibid.
10. American Library Association, Public Information Office, *America's Libraries: New Views* (Chicago: American Library Association, 1988).

SPECIAL REPORT

Ranking the Reference Books: Methodologies for Identifying "Key" Reference Sources

Richard L. Hopkins

SUMMARY. Limitations on both time and human memory make it impossible for the reference librarian or staff member to become aware of even a fraction of all the reference sources that have been published. There is, however, a small number of basic, fundamental or "key" sources that are widely used or widely recommended. In all likelihood these sources will answer a high proportion of all the questions that may appropriately be answered by published reference materials. This paper explores a number of the ways that these "key" reference sources may be identified. The author concludes that a knowledge of the types or categories of reference materials that exist and what each type will do best, along with a knowledge of a corpus of basic, fundamental or "key" reference titles, will contribute to a firm foundation for effective and efficient reference service.

There are at least three good reasons why reference librarians should be interested in knowing what the most widely used, the

Richard L. Hopkins is Assistant Professor, School of Library, Archival and Information Studies, University of B.C., Vancouver, B.C., V6T 1Y3 Canada.

141

most important, the "key" reference sources are. The first reason is simply the satisfaction of human curiosity, for surely one of the main purposes of reference librarianship, and one of its greatest pleasures, involves locating information that will answer questions that were motivated by someone's curiosity. It is the type of satisfaction we derive, for example, from learning that the ten most cited authors in the *Arts & Humanities Citation Index* for the period from 1976 to 1983 were Karl Marx (11,000 citations), Lenin (8,902), Shakespeare (8,060), Aristotle (7,745), the authors of the Bible as a group (7,035), Plato (6,904), Freud (6,111), Noam Chomsky (4,444), Hegel (4,439), and Cicero (4,386).[1]

The second reason for wanting to know what the "key" reference sources are might be termed "reference literacy." There are certain sources that *every* reference librarian needs to know, or at least to know about, if they are to be considered library literate. These terms and concepts relating to literacy, of course, are merely an extension to a specialized area of knowledge of the more general ideas developed by E.D. Hirsch Jr. in *Cultural Literacy: What Every American Needs to Know* and Hirsch, Kett and Trefil in *The Dictionary of Cultural Literacy*.[2]

The third reason for gaining a knowledge of key reference sources is a more pragmatic one. It is a reason that is both of interest and of significance to reference educators and to reference librarians charged with in-service training alike. Reference staff, both professionals and support staff, need to have a firm grasp and understanding of a basic corpus of reference materials. The main reason for this is obvious: the person working on the reference desk simply cannot afford the time to "reinvent the wheel" every time a patron asks a question. A set of routines, involving a knowledge of the reference interview, search strategies, and reference sources, must be stored in the memory in order to allow the reference worker to respond to reference questions in both an effective and an efficient manner.

Library science students, however, often complain that there are just too many reference sources to learn, and that besides every library is different and will therefore utilize a unique set of reference materials. The answer to the second part of this complaint is relatively straightforward. Even though every library has a unique clientele, and therefore perhaps a unique set of information needs and reference materials, every library also at one time or another has to go beyond the limits of its own resources in order to supply answers to questions. If the reference staff doesn't know of the existence of materials, even basic materials, other than those in its own collection, then accurate referral or interlibrary reference service becomes difficult if not impossible. Even for practical purposes, then, students will need to learn about some reference sources that they will never actually directly use themselves.

"KEY" OR BASIC REFERENCE SOURCES

The answer to the first part of the complaint is somewhat more difficult to provide, for it is true indeed that there are too many reference sources to learn in any meaningful way.

One of the first problems that the reference teacher faces, in fact, is to determine which reference sources merit attention at an introductory level out of the literally thousands of sources that have been published. Admittedly many sources, particularly those associated with a specific subject area, can be deferred to senior level courses, but that still leaves thousands of other titles to choose from. Restrictions on classroom time and human limits to the amount of information that can profitably be assimilated in a relatively short period of time, both dictate that these many sources be reduced to a manageable number.

Fortunately significant economies of effort can be achieved by focusing on the most widely used, the most important, the "key" reference sources. Bradford's Law of Scattering, an important bibliometric law, has important insights to offer here. Bradford "found that a small number of journals in a field yielded a high proportion of all the relevant articles."[3] It does not take a great leap of the imagination to project that for those reference questions that are most appropriately answered by published reference sources, a relatively small number of sources will answer a high proportion of all the questions asked (although the present author has not yet seen any empirical evidence to substantiate this).[4] This implies that the most widely used or most important general reference sources be identified at the outset of any introductory reference course. By identifying and then concentrating on two or three hundred important or "key" reference sources the reference instructor will be providing his/her students with a basic corpus of knowledge that will supply answers for the majority of reference questions, and will thereby be providing them with a solid foundation for offering both effective and efficient reference service.

The difficulty, of course, lies in deciding which reference sources are "key" sources, that is, those that are widely used or are widely regarded to be important sources. In all likelihood it is not possible to arrive at a definitive answer to this question, that is, it is not possible to compile a completely definitive list of basic reference sources. To achieve this, too many different types of data would need to be gathered and combined: for example, sales statistics, a survey of librarians in all types of libraries as to which sources they use to answer questions or which sources they consider to be important, a survey of library school instructors as to which sources they teach in basic courses, bibliometric studies of use of reference sources by scientists and scholars, etc.

The fact that a definitive answer may not be possible, of course, does not preclude attempts to arrive at answers that are less complete. Larsen, in fact, made one such attempt in 1978 when he surveyed sixty-three ALA-accredited library education programs. Faculty members responsible for teaching basic reference courses "were asked to submit syllabi or lists of the specific titles presented in their reference courses."[5] Larsen received responses from thirty-one accredited schools.

It was Larsen's survey, in fact, that stimulated an interest in one of the author's students, Arthur Coren, in a course on the literature of the arts and humanities, to explore the question of which reference books were the most widely recommended or used. The present author had devised an assignment for the course that utilized both published guides and citation indexes that would help to reveal to students the nature and structure of various subject areas in the literatures of the arts and humanities.[6] Each student in the course selected a subject area in the arts and humanities to study. Then, by examining introductory sources (guides to the literature, general encyclopedias, subject encyclopedias, handbooks, introductory monographs, etc.) the students compiled a list of recommended monographs in their field. These monographs were placed in rank order based on the number of recommendations they had received in the introductory sources. The top twenty titles were checked in all of the published volumes of the *Arts & Humanities Citation Index*. A second rank order list was then produced based on the number of citations each title had received. The final part of the assignment involved critically comparing the similarities and differences between the two lists.

PUBLISHED LISTS OF RECOMMENDED SOURCES

Coren's first task in his assignment, entitled "Key Reference Titles: Who Uses Them?", was to identify published lists of recommended reference sources. Initially he identified three such lists or sets of lists: "Landmarks of Reference," a column appearing in *Reference Services Review* (RSR) over a four year period from October/December 1980 to Winter 1983 which yielded 9 sources; "Personal Choice" or "Desert Island" (name varies), a column appearing in RSR from the Fall 1982 issue to the Summer 1987 issue, which yielded 128 sources; and "RQ 25th Anniversary List of Distinguished References," published in the Fall 1985 issue of RQ, which yielded 25 sources.

When these three lists or sets of lists were combined, only 14 sources had been mentioned by three or more commentators. These sources are listed here in rank order along with the number of times they were each recommended:

Times Atlas of the World (7)

World Almanac and Book of Facts (6)

The Bible (5)

Familiar Quotations (5)

New Grove Dictionary of Music and Musicians (5)

Oxford English Dictionary (5)

Encyclopedia of Bioethics (4)

Enclyclopedia of the World Art (4)

McGraw-Hill Encyclopedia of Science and Technology (4)

New Encyclopedia Britannica (4)

United States Government Manual (3)

Webster's Third New International Dictionary (3)

Whitaker's Almanack (3)

World Book Encyclopedia (3)

These results are interesting, but are very limited both in terms of numbers and in terms of accuracy. The present author suspects, for example, that the relatively high positions accorded to the *Times Atlas of the World* and to *The Bible* in this list of reference sources are a result of the basic premise behind the "Personal Choice/Desert Island" column, namely selecting sources to use while "stranded on a desert island" (all of the choices for these two sources did in fact come from this column).

A more satisfactory list, both in terms of number of sources and representativeness, Coren found, was the one derived from the results of Larsen's survey. This holds true even despite the fact that Larsen did not find as much agreement amongst the reference teachers about what reference sources were considered to be basic as he had anticipated. Larsen found that there were 2,014 titles when all of the sources from all thirty-one of the schools were combined, but that "only 7.3 percent of the total number are agreed upon by half or more of the schools,"[7] that is, only 147 titles were taught by 16 or more of the schools. Extending Larsen's analysis further, it was found that only 70 titles, or roughly 3.5% of the total, were taught by 23 or more of the schools (about 75% of the schools involved), and that only 20 titles, or roughly 1% of the total, were taught by 28 or more schools (about 90% of the schools). Only 7 titles were taught by all 31 of the schools: *Current Biography, Dictionary of American Biography, Encyclopedia Britannica, New York Times Index, Reader's Guide to Periodical Literature, World Almanac* and *Book of Facts,* and *World Book Encyclopedia.* Clearly, experts in the field were far from unanimous, except for a very small number of titles, on what reference titles are considered to be basic or fundamental (the 70 sources taught by 75% or more of the schools in the study are listed in rank order in Appendix A).

Coren, finally, turned to citation counting as one further type of evidence for establishing the wide use or importance of selected reference sources. In doing so he encountered a number of problems. The first of these involved selecting a representative and yet manageable list of reference sources that could be checked in the three basic citation indexes, *Science Citation Index* (SCI), *Social Sciences Citation Index* (SSCI), and *Arts & Humanities Citation Index* (AHCI).[8] It would not have been possible, given the limitations of manual searching that Coren faced, to search more than a limited number of sources in these three indexes. A representative and manageable list of twenty sources was achieved by combining the results of Larsen's survey with the results achieved by combining the three lists or sets of lists published in the reference periodicals.

A further problem that was encountered with the citation search was a result of the lack of authority control in the citation indexes. Care had to be taken that all of the variant entries for each title were counted in order to ensure a reasonable degree of accuracy.

The most serious problem with utilizing citation data to rate the importance of reference sources, however, appeared in the analysis stage. It became clear that some reference sources were cited more than others not only because of their relative importance, but also because of the nature of their content. Reference books are more likely to be cited if they need to be referred to as a documented authority for some fact or statistic (e.g., *Statistical Abstract of the United States*, etc.) or if they are substantive in nature (e.g., *New Encyclopedia Britannica*, etc.). Reference books are less likely to be cited if they are referred to for factual information that does not have to be documented or if they are not substantive in nature (e.g., *Encyclopedia of Associations, Acronyms, Initialisms and Abbreviations Dictionary*, etc.). The four citation ranking lists produced by Coren, one for *SCI*, one for *SSCI*, one for *AHCI*, and a combined list, are nevertheless interesting in their own right, and are reproduced as Appendixes B to E.

COMPARISON OF REFERENCE TEXTBOOKS

After examining Coren's study, the present author decided to extend the work in this area by attempting yet another approach to generating a basic list of widely used or important reference sources. He chose as the basis for his study four well-established textbooks that were designed for the teaching of basic or fundamental reference sources. These are in order of publication date:

Cheney, Frances Neel and Williams, Wiley J. *Fundamental Reference Sources.* 2nd ed. Chicago: American Library Association, 1980.

Hede, Agnes Ann. *Reference Readiness: A Manual for Librarians and Students.* 3rd ed. Hamden, Conn.: Library Professional Publications, 1984.

Taylor, Margaret T. and Powell, Ronald R. *Basic Reference Sources: A Self-Study Manual.* 3rd ed. Metuchen, N.J.: Scarecrow Press, 1985.

Katz, William A. *Introduction to Reference Work: Volume 1: Basic Information Sources.* 5th ed. New York: McGraw-Hill, 1987.

These four textbooks were aimed at slightly different audiences but they did nevertheless all clearly attempt to present what the authors considered to be "basic" or "fundamental" reference sources. The assumption underlying the present study was a relatively simple one: the greater the number of textbooks that listed a reference source the more fundamental or important the source was. If a reference source was listed by all four textbooks then it was considered to be more basic or important than one listed in only three texts.

The author compared the entries in the four texts by starting with the textbook that appeared to list the fewest sources (Hede) and then checked the entries in the other three texts. Once Hede was completed the author then checked the entries in the text next in terms of number of sources (Taylor and Powell) with the listings in Cheney and Williams and Katz. This methodology did not permit an accurate count of the total number of unique titles presented in all four textbooks, but this total may be fairly accurately estimated. Counting the number of sources listed in the index of Cheney and Williams, the text with the greatest number of sources, provided a total of 891 titles. Then, counting the number of titles beginning with the letter "A" in Cheney and Williams provided a total of 81 sources. Finally, counting the number of additional unique titles beginning with the letter "A" in Hede, Taylor and Powell and Katz, provided totals of 8, 11 and 24 respectively. These 43 titles represented an increase of about 53% over the 81 titles listed in Cheney and Williams. If the grand total in Cheney and Williams is multiplied by 53% this would provide an additional 472 titles to be added to the grand total (891 × 53% = 472 titles). Adding the two totals, one arrives at a final total of 1363 unique titles. One can be fairly confident, then, in saying that the four textbooks taken together list between 1300 and 1400 unique reference titles. For the sake of convenience the arbitrary figure of 1350 sources will be used for the calculations that follow.

When all of the sources had been tabulated it was found that the four texts had listed only 81 sources in common, or about 6% of the total (in Larsen's study all 31 schools could only agree on 7 sources out of 2014, less than 1% of the total). At least three texts in the present study agreed on an additional 132 sources, for an additional 10% of the total. Adding the two together, it was found that three or more of the textbooks had agreed upon 213 out of a total of 1350 sources, or about 16% of the total (in Larsen's study 75% or more of the schools had agreed upon 70 out of a total of 2014 sources, or about 3.5% of the total).

Bill Katz has asserted, in the preface to his textbook, that "there is no consensus on what constitutes 'basic'" reference titles.[9] This statement can be modified somewhat now to the more accurate observation that there appears to be an inverse relationship between consensus on basic reference titles and the number of experts or commentators involved. The greater the number of experts or commentators involved in the selection process the less agreement there is on what constitutes a corpus of basic or fundamental reference sources. One can only speculate about the reasons for this finding. First, it seems likely that every reference expert or commentator will have had a unique background of experience in reference work. Every reference title will, therefore, have had a different emphasis or importance in every commentator's previous work experience. A second factor could be that local needs or conditions will tend to increase the importance of some reference titles and will tend to diminish the importance of others.

Whatever the reasons for the fairly limited consensus, the fact is that there was more agreement amongst the four textbook commentators (all agreed on 6% of the sources, and at least 3 out of 4 agreed on 16% of the sources) than amongst the thirty-one library school instructors (all agreed on less than 1% of the sources, while 3 out of 4 agreed on 3.5% of the sources). Similar to Larsen, however, the present author expected to find an even greater degree of agreement amongst the experts in his study than he actually found. Aside from the factors discussed above, two other factors might be used to help account for the relatively low level of agreement amongst the textbook authors. The first is the fact that the texts are clearly aimed at slightly different audiences. Hede, for example, appears to place more emphasis on children's reference sources and on school library sources than the other texts; Taylor and Powell's text is designed for self-study; Cheney and Williams' text does not attempt to cover all types of reference sources; Katz observes that not "all so-called basic titles are included," because, among other reasons, "the objective of this text is to discuss various forms, and the titles used are those which best illustrate those forms."[10] A second factor that should be noted here is that the textbooks range in publication date from 1980 to 1987 and so newer reference titles by necessity will be somewhat underrepresented.

The view taken in this study, however, is that if all of these factors (different work experience of commentators, different intended audiences, and different publication dates) do indeed produce less agreement about what reference sources can be considered to be basic or fundamental, then this should be considered a positive rather than a negative outcome of the process. This is so because each source included on the final list may then be truly considered to be a basic, fundamental or "key" reference source, having withstood both the test of four independent judgments and the test of time.

The author has listed the results of the textbook study in Appendix F.[11] The reference sources have been classified and arranged in alphabetical order by type of source. Within each type those recommended by all four textbooks are listed first, followed by those sources listed by only three textbooks. Although classifying sources into groups by type may lead to some disagreement about where an individual source should be placed (is the *Statistical Abstract of the United States*, a handbook or is it a yearbook?), this arrangement was thought to be the best one for allowing readers to make useful comparisons.

COMPARISON OF RESULTS WITH LARSEN'S SURVEY

Larsen, in his study, made some attempt to summarize his results in terms of the number of titles in each category by type of reference source. Taking all 2014 titles he found that "There were 370 bibliographical information sources listed by at least one library school. The next largest categories were handbooks and indexes with 351 and 246 titles, respectively.''[12] Examining just those sources listed in his study by 23 or more schools (75% of the schools) the following approximate percentages for each category, listed in rank order, result: biographical sources (20%); indexes (16%); dictionaries (14%); bibliographies (10%); encyclopedias (10%); handbooks (7%); yearbooks (7%); geographical sources (6%); serial reference sources (6%); government publication reference sources (3%); directories (1%). The results of the present study for those sources listed by 3 or more textbooks (75% of the textbooks), provide the following approximate percentages for each category in rank order (the categories differ somewhat from those used by Larsen): bibliographies (24%); indexes/abstracts (14%); dictionaries (12%); biographical sources (12%); encyclopedias (10%); yearbooks (9%); geographical sources (5%); guides (5%); library/book trade journals (4%); handbooks (3%); directories (1%); and news services (1%).

Another comparison that can be made with Larsen's study is to note any discrepancies between the sources listed in the two studies. First, Larsen's list of 70 sources taught by 75% or more of the schools can be compared with the 213 sources listed by 75% or more of the textbooks. When this comparison is carried out there are five titles on Larsen's list that do not appear on the textbook list: *The Lincoln Library of Essential Information* (listed by only 2 texts); *Funk & Wagnall's New Standard Dictionary of the English Language* (listed by 2 texts); *Directory of American Scholars* (listed by 2 texts); *Reader's Encyclopedia* (listed by 1 text); and *World Bibliography of Bibliographies* (listed by 2 texts). The author feels that the discrepancies here can most likely be explained by the fact that the information in these five sources has become dated over time and is therefore no longer current enough to be widely recommended.

Next, the 81 titles that were included in all four textbooks can be compared with the 142 sources that were listed in Larsen's study by 50% or more of the library schools. When this comparison is carried out it is discovered that there are 17 titles on the textbook list that do not appear on Larsen's list. Four of these titles can be accounted for by the fact that they were published only a few years before Larsen's study in 1978: *6,000 Words* (1976), *Webster's Collegiate Thesaurus* (1976), *Encyclopedia Buying Guide* (1976), and

Introduction to U.S. Public Documents (1975). Several other titles were first published in the mid-to-late 1960s: *Children's Books in Print* (1969), *Subject Guide to Forthcoming Books* (1967), *Random House College Dictionary* (1968), *Merit Student's Encyclopedia* (1967), *Reader's Digest Almanac and Yearbook* (1966; an interesting question to research here would be how long it takes a reference source to become well established, especially in the relatively conservative guides to reference sources and in introductory textbooks). Five other titles, however, had been published for some considerable time: *Library of Congress Catalogs: Subject Catalog* (1950-), *Concise Oxford Dictionary of Current English* (1911-), *Webster's New World Dictionary of English Language* (1953-), *Publishers Weekly* (1872-), and *Occupational Outlook Handbook* (1949-). The only explanation for the absence of these sources from Larsen's list that makes sense is that they must have been taught and listed by fewer than half of the schools in his study. Why reference sources that have been listed by all four introductory reference textbooks, however, should be taught by less than half of the library schools surveyed must remain a puzzle.

CONCLUSIONS

Larsen, finally, concluded from his study that the tabulation of "titles currently agreed upon by reference instructors at ALA-accredited library education programs," could be useful to individual reference instructors when it came time to assess the sources they presented in basic reference courses.[13] The present author feels that the lists he has produced can be of use to both library school reference teachers and to reference librarians charged with the responsibility of in-service training of staff. He certainly, however, given the current pedagogical understandings in reference teaching, does not advocate having students learn these sources by rote memory. Instead, reference sources should be taught using the broader framework of types or categories of sources, with emphasis on what each type or category can do best, on strengths and weaknesses, etc. As Bill Katz has expressed it, "the objective . . . is to discuss various forms" of reference sources, "and the titles used are those which best illustrate those forms."[14] The present author would argue, however, that among those titles used to best illustrate different forms or types of reference materials, serious consideration should be given to utilizing those reference sources that both continue to be widely recommended and that have stood the test of time.

REFERENCES

1. Eugene Garfield, "Current Comments: The 250 Most-Cited Authors in the *Arts & Humanities Citation Index*, 1976-1983," *Current Contents* 48:3-10 (Dec. 1, 1986).

2. E.D. Hirsch, Jr., *Cultural Literacy: What Every American Needs to Know* (Boston: Houghton, 1987) and E.D. Hirsch, Jr., Joseph F. Kett and James Trefil, *The Dictionary of Cultural Literacy* (Boston: Houghton, 1988); see also Charles A. D'Aniello, "Cultural Literacy and Reference Service," *RQ* 28:370-80 (Spring 1989).

3. The *ALA Glossary of Library and Information Science*, s.v. "Bradford's Law of Scattering."

4. A news note reprinted in *The Unabashed Librarian* relates how "Dr. Herbert Goldhor at the recent LIBRARIES ON THE MOVE meeting suggested seven basic reference books that all libraries should have. They are: *World Almanac, Information Please Almanac, World Book Encyclopedia, Stevenson's Book of Quotations, An Unabridged Dictionary, A Motors Auto Repair* or *Chilton's Manual, Reader's Guide*. Dr. Goldhor," presumably with tongue firmly planted in cheek, said "that over 80% of reference questions could be answered by these basic tools." *The Unabashed Librarian* 59 (1986):24.

5. John C. Larsen, "Information Sources Currently Studied in General Reference Courses," in Bill Katz and Anne Clifford, eds., *Reference and Information Services: A New Reader*, (Metuchen, N.J.: Scarecrow Press, 1982), p. 408; originally published in *RQ* 18:341-48 (Summer 1979).

6. Richard L. Hopkins, "Perspectives on Teaching Social Science and Humanities Literatures," *Journal of Education for Library and Information Science* 28:136-51 (Fall 1987).

7. Larsen, "Information Sources Currently Studied in General Reference Courses," p. 409.

8. Coren searched *SCI* for the period from January 1980 to April 1987, *SSCI* for the period from January 1976 to August 1987, and *AHCI* for the period from January 1980 to August 1987.

9. William A. Katz, "Preface," *Introduction to Reference Work: Volume 1: Basic Information Sources*, 5th ed. (New York: McGraw-Hill, 1987), p. xii.

10. Ibid.

11. Change, it appears, is the only constant with reference books and reference publishing. For example, *Ayer Directory of Publications* is now *Gale Directory of Publications*; *Irregular Serials and Annuals* is now part of *Ulrich's International Periodicals Directory*; *Ulrich's Quarterly* is now *Bowker International Serials Database Update*; *Subject Guide to Forthcoming Books* is now part of *Forthcoming Books*; *Who's Who in Library and Information Science* has now

been superseded by *Directory of Library and Information Professionals*; *6,000 Words* has been superseded by *12,000 Words*; *Encyclopedia Buying Guide* has been superseded by *Best Encyclopedias*; *Reference and Subscription Books Reviews* is now *Reference Books Bulletin*; and *Keesing's Contemporary Archives* is now *Keesing's Record of World Events*.

12. Larsen, "Information Sources Currently Studied in General Reference Courses," p. 409.

13. Ibid., p. 416.

14. Katz, "Preface," p. xii.

APPENDIX A. LIBRARY SCHOOL STUDY

Sources Reported by 31 Schools (in alphabetical order)

Current Biography

Dictionary of American Biography

New Encyclopedia Britannica

New York Times Index

Reader's Guide to Periodical Literature

World Almanac & Book of Facts

World Book Encyclopedia

Sources Reported by 30 Schools

Biography Index

Collier's Encyclopedia

Statistical Abstract of the United States

Sources Reported by 29 Schools

Dictionary of National Biography

Encyclopedia Americana

Facts on File

New Columbia Encyclopedia

Oxford English Dictionary

Statesman's Yearbook

Webster's Biographical Dictionary

Who's Who in America

Sources Reported by 28 Schools

Book of Famous First Facts

Ulrich's International Periodicals Directory

Sources Reported by 27 Schools

Ayer Directory of Publications

Information Please Almanac

Public Affairs Information Service

Union List of Serials

Who Was Who in America

Sources Reported by 26 Schools

Bibliographic Index

Cumulative Book Index

Encyclopedia of Associations

Guiness Book of World Records

Library Literature

Lincoln Library of Essential Information

New Serials Titles

Poole's Index to Periodical Literature

Random House Dictionary of the English Language

Sources Reported by 25 Schools

Acronyms, Initialisms and Abbreviations Dictionary

Funk & Wagnall's New Standard Dictionary of the English Language

APPENDIX A (continued)

Books in Print

Columbia Lippincott Gazeteer

Compton's Encyclopedia

Contemporary Authors

Dictionary of American English on
Historical Principles

Essay & General Literature Index

Familiar Quotations

Sources Reported by 24 Schools

American Book Publishing Record

American Heritage Dictionary

Directory of American Scholars

Europa Yearbook

Granger's Index to Poetry

Reader's Encyclopedia

Sources Reported by 23 Schools

American Men and Women of Science

Dictionary of Slang and
Unconventional English

Historical Atlas (Shepherd)

Nineteenth Century Reader's Guide

Rand McNally Commercial Atlas

International Who's Who

National Union Catalog

New Century Cyclopedia of Names

Official Congressional Directory

Publisher's Trade List Annual

Webster's Second New
Dictionary of the English
Language

U.S. Government Manual

U.S. Monthly Catalog

Webster's Third New International
Dictionary of the English
Language

Whitaker's Almanack

Who's Who

Subject Guide to Books In Print

Times Atlas of the World

Webster's New Dictionary of
Synonyms

Weekly Record

World Bibliography of
Bibliographies

APPENDIX B. SCIENCE CITATION INDEX

Statistical Abstract of the United States	597 citiations
Encyclopaedia Britannica	239
Oxford English Dictionary	91
Webster's Third New International Dictionary	83
World Almanac & Book of Facts	46
Dictionary of Scientific Biography	35
Times Atlas of the World	24
McGraw-Hill Encyclopedia of Science and Technology	21
Familiar Quotations	19
World Book Encyclopedia	16
Dictionary of American Biography	15
Whitaker's Almanack	14
Who's Who in America	5
Encyclopedia of Bioethics	3
Encyclopedia of Associations	2
U.S. Government Manual	2
Acronyms, Initialisms and Abbreviations Dictionary	1
New Grove Encyclopedia of Music and Musicians	1
Contemporary Authors	0
Reader's Encyclopedia	0

APPENDIX C. SOCIAL SCIENCE CITATION INDEX

Webster's Third New International Dictionary	531 citations
Encyclopaedia Britannica	424
Statistical Abstract of the United States	424
Oxford English Dictionary	375
World Almanac & Book of Facts	165
Dictionary of American Biography	116
Familiar Quotations	73
Who's Who in America	73
Dictionary of Scientific Biography	55
U.S. Government Manual	27
World Book Encyclopedia	23
Encyclopedia of Associations	22
McGraw-Hill Encyclopedia of Science and Technology	21
Times Atlas of the World	21
Whitaker's Almanack	20
Encyclopedia of Bioethics	6
Reader's Encyclopedia	5
Contemporary Authors	4
Acronyms, Initialisms and Abbreviations Dictionary	2
New Grove Dictionary of Music and Musicians	2

APPENDIX D. ARTS & HUMANITIES CITATION INDEX

Oxford English Dictionary	242 citations
Encyclopaedia Britannica	203
Dictionary of American Biography	110
Webster's Third New International Dictionary	73
New Grove Dictionary of Music and Musicians	59
Dictionary of Scientific Biography	39
Who's Who in America	25
Familiar Quotations	24
World Almanac & Book of Facts	23
Statistical Abstract of the United States	18
Reader's Encyclopedia	10
Contemporary Authors	9
Times Atlas of the World	5
McGraw-Hill Encylopedia of Science and Technology	4
Encyclopedia of Associations	3
World Book Encyclopedia	3
Whitaker's Almanack	2
Acronyms, Initialisms and Abbreviations Dictionary	0
Encyclopedia of Bioethics	0
U.S. Government Manual	0

APPENDIX E. SCI, SSCI AND AHCI COMBINED

Statistical Abstract of the United States	1039 citations
Encyclopaedia Britannica	866
Oxford English Dictionary	708
Webster's Third New International Dictionary	687
Dictionary of American Biography	241
World Almanac & Book of Facts	234
Dictionary of Scientific Biography	129
Familiar Quotations	116
Who's Who in America	103
New Grove Dictionary of Music and Musicians	62
Times Atlas of the World	50
McGraw-Hill Encyclopedia of Science and Technology	46
World Book Encyclopedia	42
Whitaker's Almanack	36
U.S. Government Manual	29
Encyclopedia of Associations	27
Reader's Encyclopedia	15
Contemporary Authors	13
Encyclopedia of Bioethics	9
Acronyms, Initialisms and Abbreviations Dictionary	3

APPENDIX F. TEXTBOOK STUDY

Bibliographies Listed in Four Textbooks (in alphabetical order)

American Bibliography (Evans)

American Book Publishing Record

Ayer Directory of Publications

Bibliotheca Americana (Sabin)

Books in Print

Children's Books in Print

Cumulative Book Index

Irregular Serials and Annuals

Library of Congress Catalogs:
Subject Catalog

Monthly Catalog of United States
Government Publications

Monthly Checklist of State
Publications

National Index of American
Imprints Through 1800
(Shipton & Mooney)

National Union Catalog

New Serial Titles

Paperbound Books in Print

Publishers' Trade List Annual

Subject Guide to Books in Print

Subject Guide to Forthcoming
Books in Print

Ulrich's International
Periodicals Directory

Union List of Serials

United States Catalog: Books in
Print

Vertical File Index

Weekly Record

Bibliographies Listed in Three Textbooks

American Bibliography. . .1801-1819
(Shaw & Shoemaker)

American Catalogue of Books,
1861-1871 (Kelly)

American Catalogue of Books,
1876-1910

American Newspapers, 1821-1936

Audiovisual Materials (Library of
Congress)

Author-Title Index to Sabin's
Dictionary (Molnar)

Bibliotheca Americana (Roorbach)

Comprehensive Dissertation Index

Dissertation Abstracts International

British Books in Print

British Library. General
Catalogue of
Printed Books

British National Bibliography

Bureau of the Census. Catalog of
Publications

Checklist of American Imprints
For 1820-1829 (Shoemaker)

Checklist of American Imprints
For 1830-

Children's Catalog

Newspapers in Microform

Public Library Catalog

APPENDIX F (continued)

Fiction Catalog

Guide to Microforms in Print

History and Bibliography of American
Newspapers

Junior High School Library Catalog

Music: Books on Music and Sound
        Recordings (Library of Congress)

Senior High School Library
    Catalog

Standard Periodical Directory

Subject Guide to Children's Books
    in Print

Ulrich's Quarterly

Biographical Sources Listed in Four Textbooks

Biography Index

Chamber's Biographical Dictionary

Current Biography Yearbook

Dictionary of American Biography

Dictionary of National Biography

New Century Cyclopedia of Names

Webster's Biographical Dictionary

Who's Who in America

Biographical Sources Listed in Three Textbooks

American Men and Women of Science

Biography & Genealogy Master Index

Contemporary Authors

International Who's Who

New York Times Biographical Service

New York Times Obituaries Index

Twentieth Century Authors

Webster's American Biographies

Who Was Who in America

Who's Who

Who's Who Among Black Americans

Who's Who in American Art

Who's Who in American Politics

Who's Who in Library and
    Information Science

Who's Who in the World

Who's Who of American Women

World Authors, 1950-1970

Dictionaries/Wordbooks Listed in Four Textbooks

Acronyms, Initialisms and
    Abbreviations Dictionary

American Heritage Dictionary

Concise Oxford Dictionary of Current
English

Random House Dictionary of the
    English Language

Roget's International Thesaurus

6,000 Words

Webster's Collegiate Thesaurus

Dictionary of American Slang

Dictionary of Modern English Usage

Dictionary of Slang and
    Unconventional English

Oxford English Dictionary

Random House College Dictionary

Webster's New Dictionary of
    Synonyms

Webster's New World Dictionary of
    the English Language

Webster's Second New
    International Dictionary
    of the English Language

Webster's Third New International
    Dictionary of the English
    Language

Dictionaries/Wordbooks Listed in Three Textbooks

Abbreviations Dictionary

American H_ritage School Dictionary

Dictionary of American English on
    Historical Principles

Dictionary of Americanisms on
    Historical Principles

Harper Dictionary of Contemporary
    Usage

Roget's II: The New Thesaurus

Shorter Oxford English
    Dictionary

Supplement to the Oxford English
    Dictionary

Webster's New Collegiate
    Dictionary

World Book Dictionary

Directories Listed in Three Textbooks (none listed by all four)

Congressional Directory

Encyclopedia of Associations

Hotel and Motel Red Book

Encyclopedias Listed in Four Textbooks

Britannica Junior Encyclopedia

Collier's Encyclopedia

Compton's Encyclopedia and Fact Index

Encyclopedia Americana

Merit Student's Encyclopedia

New Encyclopaedia Britannica

World Book Encyclopedia

Encyclopedias Listed in Three Textbooks

Academic American Encyclopedia

Bol'shaia Sovetskaia Entsiklopediia

Brockhaus Enzyklopadie

Dictionary of American History

International Encyclopedia of the
    Social Sciences

McGraw-Hill Encyclopedia of
    Science and Technology

New Book of Knowledge

APPENDIX F (continued)

Enciclopedia Italiana

Enciclopedia Universal Illustrada Europeo-Americana

Encyclopedia of World Art

Great Soviet Encyclopedia

New Columbia Encyclopedia

New Grove Dictionary of Music and Musicians

Random House Encyclopedia

Geographical Sources Listed in Four Textbooks

Goode's World Atlas

Hammond Medallion World Atlas

National Geographic Atlas of the World

Rand McNally Commercial Atlas and Marketing Guide

Times Atlas of the World

Webster's New Geographical Dictionary

Geographical Sources Listed in Three Textbooks

American Place Names

Columbia Lippincott Gazetteer

Rand McNally Cosmopolitan World Atlas

Shepherd's Historical Atlas

Times Atlas of World History

Guides Listed in Four Textbooks

Encyclopedia Buying Guide

Introduction to United States Public Documents (Morehead)

Reader's Adviser

Guides Listed in Three Textbooks

American Reference Books Annual

Dictionary Buying Guide

Guide to Reference Books

Magazines for Libraries

New Guide to Popular Government Publications (Newsome)

Popular Guide to Government Publications (Leidy)

Walford's Guide to Reference Materials

Handbooks Listed in Four Textbooks

Bartlett's Familiar Quotations

Historical Statistics of the United States

Handbooks Listed in Three Textbooks

Famous First Facts

Guiness Book of World Records

Home Book of Quotations

Oxford Companion to English Literature

United States Government Manual

Indexes/Abstracts Listed in Four Textbooks

Library Literature

New York Times Index

Public Affairs Information
    Service

Reader's Guide to Periodical
    Literature

Indexes/Abstracts Listed in Three Textbooks

Abridged Reader's Guide

Access

American Statistics Index

Applied Science & Technology Index

Art Index

Bibliographic Index

Book Review Digest

Book Review Index

Catholic Periodical Index

Christian Science Monitor, Subject
    Index

Current Book Review Citations

Education Index

Essay & General Literature Index

General Science Index

Granger's Index to Poetry

Humanities Index

Library and Information Science
    Abstracts

Magazine Index

National Newspaper Index

Nineteenth Century Reader's Guide

Play Index

Poole's Index to
    Periodical Literature

Popular Periodical Index

Short Story Index

Social Sciences Index

Statistics Sources

Library/Book Trade Journals Listed in Four Textbooks

Publishers Weekly

Library/Book Trade Journals Listed in Three Textbooks

American Libraries

Booklist

Choice

Library Journal

Reference and Subscription Books
    Reviews

Reference Services Review

RQ

Wilson Library Bulletin

News Services Listed in Four Textbooks

Facts on File

APPENDIX F (continued)

News Services Listed in Three Textbooks

Keesing's Contemporary Archives

Yearbooks Listed in Four Textbooks

Book of the States

Britannica Book of the Year

Information Please Almanac

Occupational Outlook Handbook

Reader's Digest Almanac and Yearbook

Statesman's Yearbook

Statistical Abstract of the
    United States

Whitaker's Almanack

World Almanac & Book of Facts

Yearbooks Listed in Three Textbooks

Americana Annual

Bowker Annual

Canadian Almanac & Directory

Collier's Yearbook

County & City Databook

Europa Yearbook

Statistical Yearbook of the
    United Nations

World Book Yearbook

Yearbook of Agriculture

Refer Madness:
A Sesquilogue

Robert Franklin

By coincidence—see issue 15 of The Reference Librarian—we again found the publisher at home cutting wood. (I'm at the office a lot! he said.) His chain saw, looking light and lethal, rested on the ground near him along with a number of former tree trunks, all now logs. The Appalachian fall—a red and yellow October, with warmish days and cold nights. Good to see you again, he said while I finished patting my pockets with that lost-something feeling. I confess, I said to him, I've done so many interviews recently that since I left my notes down at the restaurant by mistake, I'm a little unclear as to what this one is about. Do you recall what I said to you on the phone that time I called?

Yeah, it was something about reference services having a "bright side"—you know, rewards for the client and a veneration for the librarian. How my name came up I don't know. I represent the crypto-schizo-cynic wing on the wonderfulness of reference service. The editor who engaged you contacted me too and asked me if I wanted to write an article or be interviewed. So I said article, and gave over a tentative title, "Refer Madness: Onlining the Hard Stuff in a Piflicated Age." On reflection I decided one needs always to fear having a title that the resulting article might not sustain . . . *Then* I realized if I said interview, I wouldn't have to do any work.

He looked at me at this point; I felt on the spot. I didn't want to agree with him. So I asked, What kind of interview would you most like to have?

Mr. Franklin is President of McFarland & Company, Inc., Publishers, Box 611, Jefferson, NC 28640.

167

One about "The Primal Reference Interview, Twixt Author and Publisher."

I'll bite. Why is that the "primal" one?

Well, it certainly defines every so-called reference interview to follow! If we (author and editor) don't collaborate to ensure there's a title index, for instance, that's it, the librarian's not going to add one to the book. If we can, by asking, catch the bibliographer in time we'd better get it annotated! Is it to have a directory? Let's be sure that's in the subtitle. If we don't get the accents right, the orthographical stickler/quester can't use the book for that narrow need. Too many flaws and even the virtues become useless.

Also, that interview is primal because it questions, What is the actual subject here? and Who needs it? What the publisher is looking for is a very well-defined subject, not one with magical mass appeal. The United States is a big place; if very plausible Joe Blow is excited about a subject, a bunch of other people probably are.

Anyway, talking to reference professionals, like we're supposed to be doing in this interview, needs a little irony to start off — most floor librarians think that *they* conduct the primal reference interview, and it's with library clientele, not authors per se and certainly not publishers. — Hey, if you want to make this interview easy, just invite me to spin out, under your benign reeling, fifteen minutes of anecdotes about negotiations with authors over inclusion criteria, uninflected serial numbering ("II.C.iv.353" — that sort of thing), combined indexing, unhorsing title hypes, lower-casing job titles, looking after the index locations of such as Messrs. Leonardo, Conan Doyle, Day Lewis, and Vaughn Williams, and much other chisling of clouds. Our duties, we publishers, are both high and low . . .

I'm not paid to make interviews easy. "Floor librarians?" I haven't heard that, I told him.

I made it up. My sister Linda and I have long agreed, it's best to just make up words or phrases whenever they're needed. Saves time for everyone, adds a little shimmer to your speech. In this belief I am briefly in league with a strain of reference bookists who make up facts, laborious as that is for many of them. It's a handy way to move ahead when trying to find out something is inconvenient. The cynic self speaks, I guess. The "piflicated age" my trial title referred to is the most cynical thing of all. Maybe we'd better not go into it . . .

Oh but I'm sure we should, I told him. The interviewer's instinct—goad them into impudence before they get their defenses built. If you can get them to say two things per page that they'll regret later, you've got a pretty good interview.

Well, education's generally pretty poor in this country—*there's* a system in entropy. And its virtual coequal, commercial television, is pretty strong all over—*there's* a system that seeks the lowest level relentlessly—and one which is, incidentally, one of the technically second-rate systems worldwide. So the people generally are pretty ignorant, at least compared to other well-off countries on earth. So they can't tell blatant untruth from exaggeration or either from slight shading, and none of those from the unvarnished truth itself. So, terrific, our professional ethic, we librarians, is that *we're* supposed to haul in the slack. We are supposed to inform the citizenry, after they've finished being informed by television (about what to buy), their classroom (to shut up and sit still), and people like Ronald Reagan (everything is just fine). And how, mainly, are we to do this? By having enormous machines idling await, packed with gobs of facts, in case the poor citizen decides to come refer instead of get on with it.

Now maybe it's o.k.—I'll shoot off in this tangent briefly—to see politicians, for instance, as of course more corrupt than normal people—and for instance to see people in the library-oriented information world as of course more selfless and truthful. But is this really true?

Well, I guess my point is, there are vast numbers of facts waiting to be referred to by a professionally-assisted member of the public, and many of those facts are innocently mistaken and many more are willfully false, incomplete, fraudulent, mislabeled, misapplied or in some cases harmful. Just like politicians crouched in beady-eyed stares at your every act of voting, information producers tensely watch your referring. And angle their actions to your fantasies and desires.

People know less now than a generation or even two ago, yet they think they know more; librarians—I'm a librarian—think they're giving them more information; vendors—I'm a vendor—

think they're virtuous and vital and probably should charge more. Businesses are way more naive than libraries, by the way; unquestionably, most would rather spend $275 a year for neat electronic packets of useless, out-of-date, unsifted and or false information than $29.95 for a simple bound volume of useless, out-of-date, unsifted and or false information. This tends to attract "the wrong kind of interest," to use the old-fashioned phrase.

And so what's this "age" that you've called "piflicated"?

That word means sort of intoxicated plus simple plus bedazzled. The American People in the late 20th century, in short. TV people.

Humans have known since Olduvai days that the manner in which a message is conveyed invests it with almost all of its status. So now we have calm, highly educated, brisk experts — librarians — hooking patrons to d*a*t*a*b*a*s*e*s, which (at no small capital outlay and no moderate maintenance cost) can, when they're "up," provide 10,000 citations to journal articles of use to you in understanding your child's eating disorder or your parent's peculiar frailty. Most of these articles are disintegrating or missing not from one's own library but from a large cooperating institution willing within reason to receive you 110 miles away.

These 10,000 citations — that's the "hard stuff" your trial title referred to?

Yeah, and there are a lot of junkies out there mainlining it, to the detriment of their family harmonies and the human race, and many librarians apparently think they'll stay clean because the jolt is going into the veins of "users," not the librarians themselves.

But we're supposed to be on the "bright side."

O.K., no problem. Information is *fun*! It's a great hobby. The neatly wrapped false stuff is just as collectible as the good stuff: probably more collectible in some cases, as the really far-out lies and deviant libels are no doubt relatively scarce in most quarters.

But that's a put-down of librarians.

Not at all. Librarians have no trick mirrors or tinted panes by which to bring in the light of information. Their (our) job is to disappear.

"Disappear?"

Yes, very much as it is the job of a typeface to disappear. You know, present no barrier between readerly eye and the insolent page. Good type design allows peruser-cruising at high speed, for extended stretches, unslowed by mannerisms like curious Q's that look like script 2's, or gargoyled serifs, or a certain fascism of strokes in words like minimum or milliliter that slams one's consciousness back into one, braking one's train. Good librarians may wear curiosities of clothing, possibly so they can be found once one enters their domain, but this probably shouldn't include sandwich boards, loud-hailers or helmet-mounted miner's lights. Metaphorically speaking . . .

So . . .

So the librarian is to buy from what's available, enable the reader to get to it, and stand out of the way thereafter. No labels on the product, no subjective signage on the shelf, no gestures on the way there, no imparting of angularity . . . If you have a problem with that, you are questioning Western Civilization, not my characterization of librarians.

Put it another way: librarians are — despite what even I've said in the past — the opposite of a "priesthood," who, at least in earlier times, jealously guarded their secrets in order to increase their income, always fearing that the populace would learn to talk to God directly (and not pay the priest to do it for them). The Protestant Reformation dealt with this; it worked.

Librarians are, to the contrary, the ones who nowadays (*some* of them) on the public behalf badger and whittle at the information guardians. But wherever humans collide they tend to collude and the librarians freely serving the public are talking about charging fees, and getting excited about expensive commercial goods. They need encouragement of the right sort to stick with their vision! Of course they need a vision too . . .

The modern era's priesthood, the legal profession, mumbling and chanting in Latin to the almighty Court, will perhaps someday suffer a revolution as well — and perhaps libraries will be the cobbled street where passionate pitchfork-wielding peasantry will play out their overthrow.

All of us have a right to expect that our librarian, at our moment of professional engagement, is *our* prepaid agent, and has no allegiance to any interest but our own.

I was involved in a real estate deal not long ago in which . . .

Exactly: whose agent *is* the realtor? The seller's alone, no matter what is said. Unavoidably librarians are agents of their suppliers (mostly vendors) — who else, for one thing, has information product? And, having bought certain items, in the fullness of professional duty, would a librarian not wish to turn to these items? Over and over? Would not the confidence of the librarian convey a sense of security to the client?

We're getting into some heavy stuff here . . .

Not really, if you approach it from a good faith point of view. The reference book or information service vendor is not a whole lot different from the librarian — both are "good guys" most of the time; society is forced to trust both about equally, and the two to trust each other the same.

If we're talking about who are "agents" of whom, where does the author fit in?

Well, the publisher is an agent of the author. This is not a razzle-dazzle, an Abbot-and-Costello of who informs whom. These are all simple truths. Slightly subtler, but still explicable with words as straightforward as those used for "publisher is author's agent," is the parallel truth that the publisher is the agent of the public, the means by which the public spirals thoughts through itself. Endlessly recycling both right thoughts and wrong ones.

But aren't these just your words painted over obviousness . . . ?

Yes and no. What I'm getting at, is, in a sophisticated culture (as in a highly evolved animal body) cause and effect are not clear; and "agency" is a tendentious notion, implying hierarchy for one thing. Many things are separate and spontaneous that look like they're connected. There's always been a lot of "coincidences" around here — the employees turn their hands into quavery spaceships and go woo-oooh like *Twilight Zone . . .*

Back to earth, and today . . .

My description of publisher as author's agent has its practical publishing-company implications — to wit, in acquisitions. Does one suppose the manuscript one is being offered right here and now adequately reflects what the public is interested in, or should one tinker and "improve" and make formalistic demands upon the author — or is it better to generate one's own ideas (based on the publisher's specialized knowledge and experience) and find authors for them? These are three significant kinds of (nonfiction) acquisitions philosophies being pursued now in the U.S.

Are you saying there are only three and these are they?

There are only about one or two other kinds, notably the sausage-grinder school textbook in which religious fanatics from Texas dictate what little may be said, and neither the committee authoring it nor the publisher can afford to care much unless psychically fascinated by the beckoning grave. These fanatics, incidentally, seem to represent a third strain of people vis-à-vis libraries: not an underclass needing but ignorant of books, not a group who wish to refer, refer, refer, eagerly, to your collection (and perhaps, intellectually, to do little else), but fatalistic know-it-alls for whom your bound volumes are at best dangerous. I prefer (being contrary is more fun) to pick on middleclass types comically immersed in "referring" — the painless, cartoonish finger of mind plunged into fanblades of data — but of course, by many powers, the fanatical strain of library disdainers are the greater peril to advancing civilization.

You were talking about acquisitions philosophies . . . Where does your company fit?

We're kinda into Zen. In this world you can either add to or you can subtract from everything you touch. (Philosophically I don't believe you can support "or leave it alone" as a third option. Not to get *too* mystical: just thinking hard about something "adds" to it.) Copy-editors are especially well-placed to learn this lesson and thus to extend its penumbra if they advance. Once you begin adding (including changing) something at the beginning of a manuscript you've imposed a new structure and taken on grave responsibility for new orders of consistency, which become complex, and weighty, as "variations" and "exceptions" begin to crop up, past page 50, past page 100, past page 200, as the editor doggedly plows onward, bending evermore with the burden, beginning to wish no change had been imposed, torn between on the one hand starting over and undoing the change — conceding both Personal Error and Wasted Money and losing face with the author who will see mess and indecision all over her manuscript — and on the other persevering in a muddy Wonderland of groundless effort, buoyed only by the egotistical belief that despite its flaws the imposed system is superior to the author's . . . These are like unto terrors in the night.

Yes, and . . .

So, the point is, we learned early at the word and sentence level, Woodsman stay thy axe! Editor, lay aside thy pen! This got us into a habit of making a handful of big decisions rather than endless series of little ones. More machete than scalpel, you could say. (Always retaining a dash of corporate egotism — "*we* can wield the machete *as if* it were a scalpel!" — just for mental health reasons.)

To get back to the point: we do acquisitions — the other end of the spectrum sentences are on — this way too, pretty much. Don't hassle authors over trivial "improvements" (Include Canadians! Start with 1945 not 1960! Put this part in alphabetical not chronological order! Add birth/death dates to each! Change "Labour Party" to "Labor" throughout!) and therefore by extension *also* don't tell them to write a different book. First of all, odds are, they know better than you do! Secondly, if you feel strongly about it (has *French* accents everywhere, so obviously needs German, Spanish and Italian put in) have your editors do it, silently and routinely, no big deal.

Do you get any feedback as to how your publishing philosophy works out?

Before I say yes, I want to add that there are extremes to everything. There are, unfortunately, some publishers who simply print *as is* whatever it is an author has supplied regardless of even gross flaws. Their Zen is greater than our Zen — and furthermore they are the wave of the future. A glimpse of the future has been available for decades in "proceedings" type volumes, in which almost everyone involved is at their most cynical: destined not to be read or "used" by anyone, published years too late (some academics can take anywhere from 20 to 45 months to turn in a print copy of their contribution), poorly written, archetypally "uneven," repetitive, indifferently — or ruinously — "edited," they are nevertheless published and hyped by publishers who know all the above negatives and employ this knowledge by raising the price, and, finally, bought by librarians so well trained to be relatively nonjudgmental that the intrinsic worth of their purchases is the least of their worries.

Now imagine two (only) changes: "proceedings" written by only one person, and published instantly. This is part of the future. Suppose "everybody" did this! You don't have a "marketplace of ideas," you have the chaos of the aftermath of explosion with dazed, anomic individuals withdrawing into themselves.

I have a fantasy image of a basketball gymnasium, packed from foul lines to rafters with noisy foot-stomping fans, in fact a thunderous din has replaced nearly everyone's consciousness (except the players'). Hundreds of hortatory chants and cheers are being voiced in groups of twos and threes and fours (half for home team, half for visiting of course). No cheerleaders or prearrangements. The confusion is just short of total, the multiplicity of barking minichoruses a dense, throbbing, Dantean surround. Then I fantasize groups here and there, moved by mysterious congruences, beginning to give way, dropping *their* chant (Gimme an Eff! Gimme a You!) to join a slightly louder or more reptile-brain-rhythmic neighbor cheer (Go, Go, Get that Ball!), both perhaps soon to yield to "Shoot shoot shoot" (my fantasy includes recognition that the simpler messages are likely to win out), and so on. Till finally the gym settles by a long series of small conquerings into two chants only (this is a contest; you can't get it below two; same as life) — Yay Cougars! and Go Big Red!

This is "publishing" through to the far future. Thousands of chants, clangoring contradictorally, all equally "valid," most destined for reverberative entropy — let's call it echo death — but a few certain special ones picking up steam . . .

Hey, far out, I said, nictitating chummily, showing I could be also wry and resonant. But, I asked him, do you ever get any sign your Zen flies?

Sure, we probably publish half a dozen books a year that arrived at our door because the tightly-wrapped Western White Man approach at a previous publishing house hadn't sat well with the author. Our Zen is greater than theirs! Our hassles are fewer, smaller, or somehow more forgivable. The reviewers (once the book is out) generally can't be trusted to tell the difference or favor the fuss-free, or even to discern the issues involved in the two approaches, but the authors sure can!

You mentioned, back a while, the primal reference interview — between author and publisher . . .

Yes. We figure that if — among the 350,000,000+ customary English-reading people who live in our market — one person writes a good book on an unusual topic, two things are likely to be true. One, absolutely no "market research" is needed to tell you that there are other people interested in the topic who will be thrilled to learn there's a *book* about it! And two, librarians will know all this and buy the book for appropriate collections. So ours with this author person are the most important reference interviews that will ever hover around his or her book; our explorations into What do you really mean? and What aspect of this are you interested in? and so on imitate in almost every way the questions that floor librarians are taught graciously to pursue with patrons. We just assign the author cosmic status as spokesperson for a tribe of the similarly interested, then ask as many questions as are needed.

I thought I saw a certain look suspended on the face of the publisher-who-does-no-market-research. He turned and moved the chain saw so it was no longer between us. It had a fine coat of sawdust all over—a mammoth, angry, bread-crumbed hors d'oeuvre ready for baking. I said, I seem to note there's more . . .

The dark side re-enters quickly at this point. All these librarians busily buying at least in part because the books exist (following sincerely the same process of thought the publisher went through) — the situation is ripe for exploitation. The good news is, the reference book business seems relatively uninfected by the insincere, so far. One sector I personally don't think much of purvey pamphlets of business statistics for hundreds of dollars each but by and large there is a certain modesty all around in the reference book business compared to tires or rock tapes. When "publishing" becomes far easier, librarians may become easier prey.

I should remind you, this is supposed to be the "bright side."

So, hey, life is more exciting when you have to pump up your alertness factor, learn to steel yourself, get your bloodstream readier for hardnosed staredowns. Deep-dyed professionals should welcome the future and its challenges. Librarians will have a harder task in the next century, and they will probably affect fewer people, not more, despite the generosities drilled in library schools, but the consequences of their acts of omission and commission may be greater.

In less than three months we'll enter the last decade of the millennium. Seems like a good time to make some predictions . . . (I'd learned in interview school that getting them to make predictions could enliven a piece that was starting to have too many big words in it.)

Well, trouble with predictions is, in a country this complex — and from my perspective throw in Canada, the U.K., Australia and N.Z. as well — you can substantiate about any trend you can invent. I mean, if there's perfectly serious scientists saying the globe is demonstrably *not* warming (polar ice, for instance, is in an era of thickening), there's contrarians proving anything (we live in a theocracy, no it's a fascist kakistocracy; our children have never been so well/so poorly educated; we're losing sight of what really counts versus our world is better and better through our focussed efforts; God is love versus "God doesn't hear the prayer of a Jew"; it's conservative to spend lives in a foreign war while it's liberal to conserve them minding our own business).

But I'm willing to say a few things: on a large note, computers and online databases are going to decline in favor, as people discover how limited yet tyrannical they are, how misleading, even false, yet uncorrectable they are. Attendant will be a renewed attention to books, with a gentle rise in CD-ROM products. On a small note, digital readouts are going to fade away, as people finally learn two things: the brain absorbs an analogue (the thermometer, the clock face, the fuel gauge) far more quickly than it does numbers, and one can with an analogue but not with a digital display instantly judge a critical change (the altimeter is suddenly 2000 feet lower, the rpm's are redlining, the timer's close to dinging) because of relative positions of a needle or indicator — with digitals one has to intellectualize the previous set of numbers and perform an addition or subtraction. At several milliseconds, say, to decide whether you're headed up or down, this could easily double one's reaction time in a pinch. Not good!

Anything less theoretical to say?

Well, back to books: I see them as very strong right through the next hundred years. People will always find them better for the lap. Researchers will still favor reference books too, particularly those they know their way around, can flip well back and forth in. I realize I'm a John Henry battling the steam-driven drill, but what has fascinated me in my adult years is discovering how often Mr. Henry is who you want and need and how often the machine merely causes more work than ever. Tell your editor the next *Reference Library* interview in a few years will be bookish fulminations against the Army Corps of Engineers!

So you don't see any big clash between books and electronic media coming up?

I see one curiosity, anyway: The researchers of many decades from now will be stymied by the paucity of primary sources from the late 20th century (and no doubt early 21st) — all that valuable detail lost because workaday ephemera were transmitted or stored electronically. The supplanting of written communications by phone calls has already — to take one narrow example — meant the entertainment industry of the 30s and 40s is easier to research than that of the 50s or 60s — and the 70s and 80s are comparatively devoid of primary sources except for the work of fanatical hobbyists impaled upon their topics with unlimited quantities of blue-lined school paper at hand: enter the McFarland "movie book" author! You can't find on the planet more authoritative individuals on fairly recent performing arts topics than the devoted amateurs who record enormous amounts of data they perhaps don't even realize *isn't* being recorded by the producers of it.

Even all the computer stuff that's been kept has proven within a decade or two to be inaccessible except with museum-piece equipment if you're lucky. The Pentagon probably owns six hundred billion trillion linear feet of electromagnetic data that will never be read again.

Was that an exaggeration?

Probably. The only one I've uttered all afternoon. Well my sweat's starting to chill and I told Cheryl I'd do her a little stove wood as well.

Almost balletically he stood, gripped my hand and plucked his chain saw from the ground. He quipped that they run through more trees, down at the office, but changed clothes less often. His hand swept through the air theatrically as I made to leave — trees and mountains for miles in every direction except up, where a hawk gyred in the endless blue. "These are all the facts a person ought to need to refer to," he said. "All the rest is vanity."